Returning to Study for a
Research Degree

Returning to Study for a Research Degree

Second Edition

Stuart Powell

 Open University Press

Open University Press
McGraw-Hill Education
McGraw-Hill House
Shoppenhangers Road
Maidenhead
Berkshire
England
SL6 2QL

email: inquiries@openup.co.uk
world wide web: www.openup.co.uk

and Two Penn Plaza, New York, NY 10121-2289, USA

First published 1999

Extended and revised edition 2008

Copyright © Stuart Powell 2008

A catalogue record of this book is available from the British Library

ISBN-13: 978 0 335 23351 9 (hb)   978 0 335 23353 3 (pb)
ISBN-10: 0 335 23351 1 (hb)   0 335 23353 8 (pb)

Library of Congress Cataloging-in-Publication Data
CIP data applied for

Typeset by RefineCatch Limited, Bungay, Suffolk
Printed in the UK by Bell and Bain Ltd, Glasgow

The **McGraw-Hill** Companies

For my good friend Eleanor Sheppard
(1994–2006)

Contents

11 Conclusion

Preface

Returning to study for a research degree should be a challenging and rewarding experience but it also has the potential to be daunting and even intimidating. The aim of this book is to help you make the most of your research programme, to balance the difficult juggling act of study, work, leisure and family life, and where applicable to draw upon insights and experience from any professional background that you may have to support your academic work about research.

One of the problems I faced when writing the book was how to encompass the kinds of concerns that emanate from within the range of disciplines within which research degree study is offered in the UK and indeed the kinds and levels of research degree award that are on offer. I made a decision early on that I would try to encompass all, in part because of the need to reach a large enough audience, but also because in my own work in the research degree field I have come to value very much the cross-fertilization of ideas and understandings that comes from bringing together students and supervisors from the full range of intellectual areas. I think that this bringing together can lead to richness of experience for all concerned and helps to obviate the narrowness of view that can creep in when those working within an individual discipline begin to conceive of themselves as increasingly different from those in the rest of the academic world and as having increasingly less in common in terms of standards, processes and procedures. Through my own work with research degree students and their supervisors I have come to realize that, though different disciplines and professional backgrounds make different demands on students, common problems exist and similar solutions can be suggested. I have then quite deliberately included student feedback from a range of intellectual areas and I have aimed for generality of comment on a number of occasions while striving not to lose relevance.

I have also tried to draw connections to professional backgrounds for those returning students who come from such contexts. Clearly, this will be the case for those studying within professional doctoral programmes but it may apply to many other readers as well. My strategy therefore has been to make reference where it seems appropriate and to include specific sections when necessary. Again, my intention has been to encompass the needs of a wide range of readership but in so doing I have tried not to include text in a way that may feel intrusive to those readers for whom professional matters are not relevant.

The general ideas and specific strategies that have been included in the book come from various sources: first, from my own experiences of being a research student and later a supervisor and later still a trainer of supervisors and a director of research degrees at my own university, second, from the reported experiences of my own students and those I have worked with on generic training course, and third, the experiences of supervisors I have been involved with in workshops both in my university and across the UK. Where I have included student responses these were reported either verbally or in written evaluations and feedback. You will find feedback from nurses, teachers, lawyers, graphic designers, town planners, psychologists and many more.

The original proposal for this book, which went through the usual stages of review and publisher's comment, included the notion that supervisors should be included in the overall intended readership of the book alongside their students and there was a stated intention to direct comments at supervisors periodically through the text. This intention was excluded during the process of review, in order to maintain an undiluted focus on the perceptions and needs of research degree students; however, I hope supervisors may be able to make use of the sections in this book, first, as a resource to use directly with their students, and second, as a lens through which to better understand the experience of research degree study from the perspective of the student.

Finally, my own research has led me to two understandings that underpin this book: first, that a successful return to study for a research degree in the UK requires substantial critical reflection on the part of the student, and second, that success should be interpreted, in part at least, in terms of increased ability to think effectively and critically about research as well as in terms of increased amounts of research knowledge and research skills. As a returning student you will need to learn about research through the doing of research and this book aims to help you to accommodate to this need in such a way that your return will be both successful and enjoyable.

Acknowledgements

I am grateful to all those research students from various disciplines studying for different awards who gave particular comments on some of the ideas and tasks in this book. Also, I would like to acknowledge all the research students I have had the pleasure of working with over the years and whose experiences have informed the writing of this book.

1

Introduction

Overview • Introduction • Reasons for returning to study • Interpreting learning • Summary • Conclusion

> *Some people study all their life and at their death they have learned everything except how to think.*
>
> François-Urbain Domergue (1745–1810), quoted in
> Parnes et al. (1977: 52)

Overview

This chapter demonstrates the importance of thinking about your reasons for returning to study at research degree level and what you can and should expect from this experience of a new kind of learning. It signposts later chapters where you will be able to consider the particular strategies that may help you to function more effectively as a research degree student.

In this chapter, I am working on the basis that having good reasons for returning to study, and specifically to study through and about research, may sustain you if times become difficult. I am proposing that one of the ways to get the most out of an experience of research degree study is to be as aware as possible of ways in which the very notion of learning about research and extending knowledge through research can be interpreted and that, at a more pragmatic level, when and where to study and research can be as important for the adult learner as some of the more detailed learning strategies. I explore with you personal and professional motivations and ways of sustaining interest and commitment.

In this chapter, therefore, you will be asked to:

- identify your own reasons for returning to study and the implications of those reasons
- begin to identify your own reasons for choosing research degree study specifically
- examine your own interpretations of what counts as learning and learning through and about research
- examine your own understanding what marks out research degree study as distinctive from all other forms of university study (with signposting to Chapter 2, where this issue is dealt with in more detail)
- think about questions of 'new' study and your existing lifestyle
- make connections between existing skills and those required by research degree study.

Introduction

The quote taken from Domergue at the head of this chapter suggests that a distinction can be drawn between the act of study and consequent learning and thinking. This chapter sets the scene for what follows in the book by suggesting that there is more to your successful return to study than simply finding ways of coping with a new kind of workload and so on. Certainly, the pragmatics of how to go about research degree study are important but I hope to persuade you that a significant underlying purpose of your study is to improve your abilities as a thinker and hence as a potential learner and researcher in future situations. Here I ask you to accept that the accumulation of knowledge is one interpretation of learning but it is not the only one and my suggestion to you is that it may well be an interpretation that is confining rather than liberating particularly in the context of research degree study.

Modern rhetoric calls for 'lifelong learning'; Domergue reminds us that such an endeavour is likely to remain sterile without improvement to the powers of thinking. My suggestion here is that your focus needs to be on your own ways of learning, your style as a thinker and your developing abilities as a researcher.

In order to achieve a research degree award you need not only to make a contribution to knowledge (at whatever level you are operating) but also to give evidence that you have the skills and abilities to continue to do so in an independent and self-sustaining way. We will explore this additional aspect as it relates to research degree study in more detail in Chapter 2.

Reasons for returning to study

Identifying reasons

In my own life I have returned to study twice: first, to study for an in-service degree, and second, to study for a research degree. The motivations differed on the two occasions. On the second return I had developed an intellectual interest in specific topics within my own professional practice and wanted the chance to explore them directly and in more depth. I also wanted another challenge that was at a higher (academic/intellectual) level to that already achieved. Undertaking a research degree seemed to answer both motivations – the chance to find out more coupled with a testing of my abilities. On reflection now I think that I did not fully understand that the research degree demanded more than just 'finding out', that it would require me to make a contribution to specific aspects of the field within which I was studying. Of course, 'finding out' necessarily implies that something new will be discovered or revealed but I think that I had underestimated how much attention I would need to pay to shaping my findings into a contribution from which others might benefit and learn. I think it is fair to say that when I started out on my own research degree, the thought that I might add to the substantive knowledge that was extant at the time in my professional world was beyond my expectations; it was only as I progressed that I realized the 'step-up' that was required of me, from active learner about things to a contributor to knowledge and understanding from whom others might learn. I will return to this step-up in Chapter 2 and try there to unpick what it means in terms of your study and what the longer-term implications are for you as a learner.

You will have your own reasons for returning to study for a research degree and possibly your own set of anxieties. Your reasons may relate to career advancement, or to a need to prove to yourself that 'you can do it', or to compete with colleagues, or because your employer feels you ought to get more qualifications. On the other hand it may be that you have quite simply always wanted to engage in further study but have, for one reason or another, never had the chance. You may have an intellectual interest in a specific topic and doing a research degree attracts you as a way of getting support and structure for your researching about that topic.

I suppose I went back into studying and for a research degree in particular because I wanted to find out more about how my particular kind of architecture can be progressed using new, non-traditional materials. You can read about it of course but I had some ideas of my own that I wanted to test out. Just designing buildings was not quite enough, I wanted to figure out why I believed as I did and what I was doing and how I could push the boundaries of non-traditional materials that bit further.

(Architect undertaking a doctorate in architecture)

It would be improper of me to impose my own view and suggest the kind of reason you should have for returning to study. Yet it has been a feature of discussions with research degree students at the end of research programmes that they often mention, obliquely, self-improvement in terms of their own intellectual ability but seem embarrassed to come out and say that they think they have become a better person or a person who has increased in cleverness. They do, however, sometimes admit to feeling better able to think clearly about issues, solve problems effectively, convey their views more accurately and confidently and so on. Importantly, some indicate that they feel able to contribute to their profession in a way that they did not prior to their programme of research study; indeed, some feel obligated so to do. Therefore it seems reasonable to suggest that 'learning how to think' is a distinct possibility and might well be a legitimate part of your agenda (this topic is addressed in this book in the various sections on critical thinking).

> I think that doing the PhD taught me how to research into my practice in a way that I would never have learnt from courses and workshops and so on; and I don't think just practising for years would have done me as much good either. Doing a doctorate changed me from a doer to a thinker and a doer. I know that must sound a bit pompous but I am much more reflective now in my practice. I understand how to weigh up possibilities and risks and how to devise new solutions where before I tended to follow the kinds of guidelines I picked up in my training. Now I create solutions and I find it easier to advise colleagues on courses of action and ways of exploring possibilities. I think I was always good technically but now I can think outside the box and I'm more than a good technician somehow. Sorry if that sounds arrogant.
>
> (Dental surgeon having completed a medical doctorate (MD))

Planning for study

In order to fit research study into an existing lifestyle it may help if you raise your awareness of how your time is spent at present, perhaps by listing the typical chronology of daily events or representing them diagrammatically. Such awareness of how time is spent may lead you to ways of controlling the way in which you make use of the time that you have available. One of the students (a lawyer) who commented on some of the ideas in this book described the way in which he tried not to let studying time affect what he saw as the balance of his professional work by '*studying in "dead time", e.g. on train journeys, in waiting times and lunch breaks*'. A medical engineer who had returned to study after a number of years in his profession, described the way in which he carried out the computational side of his work during the day, '*i.e. modelling/simulation/implementation*' because he did not have sufficient resources at home – in the evening he wrote up his work in such a way that he was able eventually to '*assemble it into my doctoral submission*'. He recognized that the needs of the various tasks within his research programme to some extent drove the way in which he structured his day and he acknowledged that the more he came to understand this the clearer his planning became. Clearly then, having listed or drawn the outline of your daily schedule you still need to decide how to make the necessary adjustments, but at least now you may have a clearer view of what those adjustments are.

Switching tasks and keeping track

Switching from one task to another may be a feature of life for you as a professional returning to study inasmuch as work, home and study will inevitably impact on each other. However, there may also be a case for some planned switching between tasks. In terms of knowing yourself and your preferred learning style and habits it is useful to focus upon when you need to switch between activities to prevent boredom and lack of concentration. Deliberately switching from one activity to another may be a productive device for some people in some circumstances but you may find it helpful to try to finish a previously defined step of a task before going on to something else. I find in my own work that returning to a task which was left 'in the air' means that I end up having to reorientate myself to the task; clearly this takes time which could have been more profitably used. It may be, of course, that you can devise ways of reminding yourself of just where you got to and what you were about to do (using yellow 'stickies' covered in self-directed comment is a common device).

Task: keeping track

What devices or tactics can you imagine being able to use to keep track of where you have got to with particular tasks (e.g. the assembling of some complex data sets)?

Personally I set myself milestones, such that by a particular date I will have achieved the task I set out to do.

(Medical engineer embarking on an engineering doctorate (EngD))

I work on a word-processor and I always type a comment to myself at the start of a file to remind myself what I have done and what I was going to do next.

(Librarian doing a masters in research (MRes) by way of preparation for a PhD)

I carry things in my head and write analytical memos which I don't refer to again.

(Nurse doing a masters by research in nursing management)

Self-evaluation of targets set by self, establish a work plan set by self, seek feedback from supervisor, have a research buddy to share work programmes and keep each other motivated and on task.
(Education consultant about to submit for an education doctorate (EdD))

Diary on PC.
(IT technician completing an MSc by research)

Range of activities involved in research degree study

One thing you can be sure about is that your research programme will involve you in more than simply reading books, writing essays or carrying out experiments. The range of activities that you *may* need to engage in when studying for a research degree is illustrated by the list below (clearly not all will apply to everyone because the nature of research is diffuse):

- Listening to lectures or research presentations
- Asking questions and discussing issues with colleagues and fellow researchers
- Joining in seminar discussions
- Reading books, journal articles, technical reports, reviews, doctoral theses
- Engaging in role play
- Writing notes and using them subsequently in the preparation of research reports and final submissions
- Interviewing people
- Learning key ideas, deciding what is important and what is not, deciding what is a valid research question
- Asking research questions, deciding which of any responses/answers/outcomes you receive have been useful and why
- Answering questions
- Carrying out experimental work
- Preparing for oral examination
- Reflecting on things learnt and things discovered and on things that remain to be learnt and understood
- Working out how people from different disciplines view problems in different ways and how people from different disciplines may be able to use your ideas and findings
- Considering the effects of increased understanding on your professional practice or your personal life.

The list above is not intended to be exhaustive, but merely illustrative of the range of things that are you may encounter in your studies. Neither is the list intended to be frightening; you should not feel daunted but rather encouraged. The point here is that different aspects of research degree study will require different things of you in terms of time and place and kind and level of effort. Many of the topics listed above will be returned to later in the book.

Suggestions for further reading

Of course there is no substitute for hard work but some of the shortcuts to making sure that the hard work you do is the right hard work can be found in the publications listed in Sections 1 and 8 of Further Reading.

Interpreting learning

Concepts of learning

What people value about learning and researching, and the kinds of things they assume make someone a 'learned person' and a 'researcher', will vary over time and between cultures. For example, in a Stone Age setting an understanding of the difference between poisonous and non-poisonous berries might be of vital significance and hence a valued thing to test out and learn but it may be less useful in a modern-day town. Testing out the poisonous qualities of any new plants encountered by relying on human taste might be a reasonable and legitimate form of research in the Stone Age but less so when there are established ways of testing for poison using chemical reaction. Things to be learnt, ways of learning them, ways of assessing them and ways of inquiring about them are not absolute; they are liable to change across cultures and across time.

My example of a Stone Age culture may seem a little extreme but it only extends what may be a reality for you, namely that if you have spent much time away from the world of academia or have crossed cultural boundaries then you may find that notions of what is deemed worthwhile knowledge, and what it is to study and to learn and extend that knowledge, have shifted. A clear example within current academic environments is that the memorizing of text and facts may be more highly valued in some contexts and cultures than in others (and indeed such memorizing was valued within aspects of the UK education system of the 1960s and 1970s much more so than it is today). Similarly, it is worth noting that while the ability to remember facts may be seen as necessary for the examination of learning at secondary school (e.g. at Advanced level), at PhD level in the UK candidates are usually permitted to take their thesis into the oral examination and refer to it when questioned rather than be expected to remember all that they wrote, i.e. the value of memorizing is not constant throughout educational contexts.

In a different though related context, it is also a recognized phenomenon that attitudes to 'learning from a master' and to the usefulness of copying with intellectual reverence the words and ideas of respected academic 'elders' vary across cultures. In many eastern cultures respectful imitation of accepted ideas may be required of the aspiring student whereas in western cultures that same respectful imitation may be interpreted as 'uncritical acceptance' at best and plagiarism at worst. This cross-cultural difference is returned to later in this book but here I need to stress that conceptual understanding of, and hence attitudes towards, study in general and research study in particular vary across cultural boundaries. The variations can be profound and far reaching and the impact on the unsuspecting research student can therefore be significant.

> I just did not understand that I could challenge what my tutor said. I had been brought up all my life not to question what my teachers told me. All of a sudden, and without any warning or explanation, not only was I allowed to question but I was expected to challenge and come up with my own interpretations of what was in the textbooks and then later what my data meant. Actually, I was criticized for not questioning vigorously enough. I went from being a good student who always scored the highest grades in class to a second rate student who was simply 'not up to scratch' (and here I quote the words of one of my early tutors in the UK) because I did not express my own ideas and argue for them. It was very hard for me. Even now that I have got my PhD I cannot really get used to the notion of challenging other people's ideas. But my research supervisor was very good with me, when he eventually understood just how difficult it was for me – he said I would have to 'unlearn' how I used to behave as a student (I always remember that phrase – 'unlearn') and he would help me. He did help me, by constantly making me question things in our work. He would joke about it. But I still find it difficult. I got used to it – but only really with him because it became a kind of game between us. But as soon as I was somewhere else – in someone else's research seminar or something, I slipped back into my own ways. It's hard to unlearn all those years of learning to be a respectful student.
>
> (PhD student, originally from the Republic of China, having completed his doctorate within bioscience)

Depending on your own circumstances you need to be prepared for values to have shifted, not only across cultural borders but also over time, and to be on the lookout for signs (e.g. in research degree documentation and in the attitudes of supervisors) that different kinds of knowledge and skills are being valued and different kinds of learning outcomes and skills and abilities are therefore being targeted.

Professional awareness

Clearly not all readers of this book will consider themselves to be 'professionals'. Yet many of you will be working within a professional context and returning to study full-time (e.g. via leave of absence or secondment) or part-time (often, though not always, with some recognition from your employers that time is to be spent on study). Indeed some will be engaged in a professional doctorate of one kind or another. Because of this linkage with the professions, which may be common if not universal, I include here (and indeed throughout this book) some reference to how research degree study may impact upon the professional work of the student and vice versa.

In considering different conceptions of learning we need to consider ways in which learning gains for you as a professional may occur. Wrapped up in the notion of being a professional is the concept that you will seek self-improvement, that there will be a continuous sense of you learning more about your working environment and thereby becoming more effective within it. When you re-enter study at any level then, you may have an agenda which includes the idea that study is valuable inasmuch as it contributes to your own professional performance. When you enter at research degree level it is arguable that you should develop an agenda that includes the notion that not only will your professional performance be enhanced but also you will be able to contribute to a better understanding of specific aspects of your chosen profession from which colleagues may, in turn, benefit. While it may be natural for you, and perhaps your employers, to have a legitimate expectation of professional gain from your return to study at research degree level, equally it may be ill-advised to expect that gain to be clearly defined at the outset, apparent throughout and direct, for example in terms of specific learning and research outcomes leading to specific aspects of increased effectiveness. The course of real research rarely runs true and invariably involves some sense of risk (I return to the kinds of risk involved in following chapters). In short, research programmes do not always have a clear-cut pay-off that can be determined at the outset of the work however desirable that may be for funders and supporters of the research.

What is clear is that, if you are a member of a profession, you will undoubtedly bring skills and expertise from your working practice that can be adapted to the academic environment of research degree study. It may well not always be possible to scope out what those skills are when you are not sure of exactly what this new environment entails and hence requires of you. But as your programme of study unfolds you perhaps need to keep in mind that you do have skills as a professional – some may not be dressed up as formal research skills and understandings but it may help your confidence if you try to make out the connections between your professional work and the research practice expected within a research degree.

Task: listing existing skills

List some skills that you practise within your professional work (or in your life outside academia) that you think, at this stage, may be of some use to you in undertaking a research degree.

Note: clearly, if you complete this task at the outset of your studies then your list will represent your expectations rather than your experience of the study itself, nevertheless it seems useful at such a stage to review the battery of skills that you do possess and which may therefore be called upon. The list can of course be reviewed as your programme of study develops.

Summary

- You have considered your reasons for returning to study.
- You have examined your interpretations of learning and contemplated pragmatic questions of how to create the conditions most likely to produce effective learning for yourself during the course of your studies.
- You have seen that 'returning to study' is a process necessarily involving change to you as learner.
- You have considered the notion that research degree study is of a particular kind (this issue is revisited throughout the book and in Chapter 2 in particular).

Conclusion

You have chosen to return to study at research degree level and you need now to reconcile yourself to the implications of that choice. I have suggested that a useful text to take to heart would be the quote from Domergue with which the chapter opened. I have implied that you might choose to underpin your interpretation of your own return to study as an opportunity to improve your ability to think and learn rather than merely as a time to accumulate knowledge, skills or even simply good grades. In particular, returning at research degree level carries with it the implication that you will have to add to the sum total of knowledge in your area and not simply learn more about what is currently the extant state of knowledge.

2

Researching and learning

> *A thinker sees his own actions as experiments and questions – as attempts to find
> out something. Success and failure are for him answers above all.*
> Friedrich Nietzsche (1844–1900), *The Gay Science*, Section 41 (1882)

Overview

This chapter deals directly with the distinguishing features of research degree study and the distinctive demands it places upon, and potential rewards it gives to, you as a student returning to study. The relationship between your researching and your professional practice (where that is relevant) is explored as well as that between your studying and your researching. You will be asked, for example, to reflect upon your studying about research (e.g. about the broad approaches to investigation you might take and specific methods of seeking evidence that you might employ) and your studying through research (e.g. studying your professional practice through acting upon it in an investigative way and changing it in the process). In this chapter, therefore, you will be asked to:

- distinguish research degree study from other kinds of academic study
- come to terms with differing notions of

  - curriculum
  - investigation
  - level of critical analysis
  - self-direction (in terms of research and study)
  - desired outcomes of study.

Introduction

Research is sometimes interpreted as something that is special and is done by professional researchers and which may or may not be of benefit to society at large. Study on the other hand may be seen as something one does for one's own sake, in order to learn something for whatever reason or because learning it leads to something else such as an academic award. A broader interpretation of research is that it is something that is done by many different kinds of person, including children in primary school and workers in all walks of life. What is of interest to us here is the way in which research can become the target of your activity ('I will research this topic'), the thing you learn to do ('I will learn about researching') and also the mode of study through which an academic award can be gained ('I will learn about researching, and hence gain my award, through the process of doing it'). In the sections that follow I will try to explore the relationships between researching and learning as they are manifest within the context of research degree study.

Perhaps what is most important to stress is that this new form of study (through research) requires that you take the stance of the 'thinker' as reflected in the quotation from Nietzsche that opens this chapter. I am encouraging you to see what you do in academic terms (be it reading, writing, listening etc.) primarily as experimentation and questioning. What matters from this form of study, is that you learn to think in this way rather than that you learn any one thing or set of things.

What differentiates research degree study?

Undergraduate and taught postgraduate study

It may be a truism to say that students go to university to learn things and that therefore a prime purpose of universities is to enable or facilitate that learning. In the case of undergraduates, programme committees meet and decide, before the students are even recruited to the course, what content will be on offer; decisions are made about just what those students who enrol at the start of term will learn as they study for their degrees and hence just what they will be assessed upon. Indeed, recruitment is based on universities setting out their stalls in terms of what they will teach (and increasingly 'how' the material will be taught) and students 'signing up' on the basis of what is spread out before them. There is then an established relationship between undergraduate student, university, academic staff, curriculum and assessment structure that contains an amount of predetermination. Things become a lot less clear at postgraduate 'taught' level where final dissertations may involve investigation which, to some degree, allow postgraduate students to begin to carve out their own areas of focus within a broad disciplinary field. However, it is the case that even here, in this postgraduate taught domain, to a greater or lesser extent what is to be learnt is predetermined and relates to existing knowledge.

The step-up to research degree level

To me the significant step-up to research degree level relates to the shift from learning more about what is already known, to learning the appropriate processes that enable you to find out things that were not previously known and then demonstrating that you have learnt these processes by proceeding to find out things that were not previously known or were not accepted understandings. In short, you have to move from absorbing existing knowledge, skills and understandings so as to make yourself a more knowledgeable and skilled person who understands the world effectively to someone who is able to generate new knowledge and skills or bring about new understandings of the world. Of course there are levels with the general level of research degree study – ranging from masters to higher doctoral – and I return to these distinctions in Chapter 3.

> I feel that I know enough about structural engineering now to be able to start doing some projects for myself – some testing out of materials that I think have potential for use in my field that, at the moment, are only used in a limited way elsewhere.
>
> (Structural engineer applying for an EngD programme)

One signifier of the step-up that I note above is that a new level of critical analysis is required from you as a research degree student. It is not enough any more to be in command of the facts and to be able to deploy intellectual skills; now there is a need to develop a critical acuity in relation to the issues that arise in your studies. You need to be able to challenge the 'known' and question the accepted in a way that combines reason with intellectual scepticism. Here I do not mean that you need to be merely critical in its more restricted sense (e.g. of criticizing everything irrespective of its substance or merit) but rather that you need to be conscious of the argument that underpins what is being said to you or that you are reading and able to unpick the soundness of that argument in terms of the levels of evidence presented and the appropriateness of the conclusions that are being drawn through the argument and based upon the evidence.

There are two potential pitfalls facing you as a student returning to study at research degree level. First, you should not confuse what was required of you on taught university courses with what is required at research degree level. There is a distinct and important difference as I have tried to delineate above. Second, you would be unwise to see this step-up as an impossible one for you to achieve. 'Discovering' new knowledge in your field may seem a daunting if not impossible task but in reality what is required typically by university regulations is that you shape new understandings or enable reconsideration of existing views of the world. There are levels within the field of research degrees that will necessarily require differing levels of contribution in the senses defined above. With reference to the PhD specifically, within the constraints of, typically, three or four years of full-time study (or its part-time equivalent) we are most probably talking about readjusting or pushing back the boundaries of knowledge rather than discovering something of earth shattering significance and wholly new. Again, it is a matter of referring to the specific wording of the criteria for the award as applied in your chosen university.

Task: challenging the commonly accepted

- Note down one accepted 'truth' in your research discipline or profession (e.g. an accepted way of doing things or a common belief about a substantive matter of concern to you).
- Is there anything about that 'truth' that you think is worth challenging (e.g. which may seem to you to be not necessarily the case)?
- How might you go about making such a challenge (e.g. is there any way of testing things out to question the validity of what is commonly accepted)?

There is a lot of published analysis of the author I am interested in researching that suggests that much of the impetus for his writing stems from his struggles with his own sexuality. But I am not at all sure this is the case. It seems to me that he may well have been quite happy with his sexuality and that our suppositions that it must have been a struggle are based on our own feelings rather than his. In other words we are projecting onto him. I want to look through his diaries and letters for signs of this 'struggle'.

(Librarian doing a masters in research (MRes) by way of preparation for a PhD)

Conventional wisdom would have it that children of all abilities need to be educated together if we are to have a truly integrated society. What

I'd like to do is to test this out by doing an international comparison of attitudes in societies with different kinds of approach to segregation, integration and special schooling.

(Head teacher studying for an education doctorate (EdD))

The student as driver of research degree study

The next distinction relates to who drives the decision making as to what should be studied and researched and how research study should be undertaken. In short, who decides what areas are to be investigated and how that investigation should most effectively and reliably be carried out? As I have already noted, in taught course work, it is typically committees that decide on content and tutors who deliver it. In research degree study the emphasis shifts, though the institution retains a significant role. The student now has a much more prominent role in deciding what will be studied and how. Indeed, in many universities, at PhD level in particular (what is written below applies to a lesser extent to masters and MPhil levels) the student drives decision making with regard to when research work will be submitted for assessment (within institutional regulations regarding time frames etc.). This last point is worth emphasizing because it underlines the important role that the research student takes in terms of ownership of the direction of the work. In most universities the student is required to know when he or she has made the necessary 'contribution' and is therefore ready to submit for assessment. It is also worth noting here that this situation, where the student takes control of the process, is not universal outside of the borders of the UK. In many other countries, supervisors and awarding committees have a much stronger role to play.

I have two reasons for mentioning the particularity of the UK system. First, it is important that, if you are a student from overseas, you realize that norms and procedures that exist in your home country might not exist in the UK. A UK research degree is awarded according to UK expectations. I make no value judgement here – I am certainly not saying UK awards are better – but they are distinctive and you will be examined according to UK perceptions of what counts as, for example, 'doctoral' (see Chapter 3). Second, in the UK system, at doctoral level in particular (and to a lesser extent at masters and MPhil levels), the student needs to see him/herself as the initiator of work and hence as someone who 'owns' the programme of study. Of course this sense of ownership and control is something that develops over a period of time and it may seem to those setting out on a research degree registration that to know enough and be skilful enough to be able to truly drive forward the project independently is beyond their capabilities. Such feelings are common and quite reasonable – but the whole point of research degree study is that you *will* become an independent researcher capable of designing, carrying out and reporting successfully research programmes in your field. So, if you are starting out on a research degree programme then you need to be thinking about how you can develop the kinds of independence that will enable you to meet the criteria for the award.

Of course your supervisor can guide you but at the end of the day it is your project, you will have to submit for assessment and you will have to answer the questions that the examiners choose to ask you in order to make a judgement as to whether or not you have demonstrated that you have met the criteria for the award. The only caveat I need to make here is that there is disciplinary variation in terms of how 'independence' is interpreted. In some of the physical sciences in particular, students may be recruited to work on projects already defined and developed by established academics who have, for example, successfully been awarded research grants. Here then the process of taking ownership and taking initiative may be qualitatively different but the need at the end point – to be an independent researcher capable of designing your own (successful) research projects, remains.

The usual procedure therefore falls into three main stages: registration, progression and examination.

Registration

You as a research student will be required to develop, in collaboration with your supervisor, a research programme that will be robust enough, in terms of aims and methodologies, to lead to 'findings' (you may need to interpret this term very broadly) that will be commensurate with the level at which you are operating (doctoral, MPhil or masters). Of course, the key variable in here is the term 'in collaboration' – it can mean a variety of forms of consultation and negotiation; according to discipline and local circumstance you as a student will be more or less truly collaborating with your supervisor(s). My suggestion is that you need to play as full a part in that process of collaboration as is possible. You need to take ownership of the project (or your part of it) sooner or later and in my view the sooner the better – certainly the great danger is that you never truly take control and begin to drive the work forward and then you may find yourself in a position where you need to submit for an award that requires you to be able to argue and defend your research work as an independent researcher should and yet you have no experience of doing that.

Progression (sometimes referred to as 'transfer')

If you are studying at doctoral level there will be at least one point within your studies where you will be required to submit work to date and a plan of work to be completed before submission (or to the next stage, in more complex systems). This may be described as 'transferring' registration from MPhil to PhD or it may be a matter of 'progressing' from one phase of study to another (e.g. annual). Whatever system your institution employs, you will have a significant role in describing to assessors what you have done and defining what you believe you need to do in the next phase. You will most probably be required to explain and justify these summaries of work done and projections of work to come either in a discursive document or in front of a panel of one sort or another. Again, what the assessors will be looking for is evidence that you have taken, or are taking, control over the research programme.

Examination

As already noted, you as a student will be expected to know when you have 'done enough' simply because you will be expected to know other work in the field in the sense that you will know what others have already found out within your topic area and what is therefore published and hence you will be able to judge whether or not your work has 'made a contribution'.

Purpose of the different levels of research degree award

All research degrees awards are gained, in part or in whole, by doing research. They are all supervised rather than taught. Though they may include some taught components, they are awarded for meeting defined criteria rather than for following a curriculum. They are all open to public scrutiny inasmuch as the results of the research are usually 'published' either through normal publication channels or made available through university libraries and/or the British Library. However, the different research degree awards have different origins and different purposes, which I summarize here simply to give you an idea of where your own target award fits in terms of the national portfolio of research degree study.

- The doctorate in the UK has its origins in the thirteenth century and was originally a training for an academic career. That raison d'être persists but the purposes of the award now encompass a research career in academia (rather than a career in academia as a whole), training for research in the world at large, training for high level work in a profession and of course may be undertaken from the perspective of curiosity driven research for its own sake.
- Professional doctorates relate more to mid-career development and updating, to the gaining of advanced professional recognition (and in the case of the doctor of clinical psychology (DClinPsy) the award is a licence to practise). They tend to be cohort-based and the outputs are, typically, theses in addition to course work or projects.
- Practice-based doctorates are generally located within the arts and design, where outputs may be, for example, art-works, artefacts or compositions.

- The PhD by published work again relates largely to mid- to late career researchers with an existing research portfolio.
- The MRes and the other research masters (e.g. MSc/MA by research) offer a research training and, as well as having self-standing value, may be treated as preparatory awards for doctoral registration or as an indicator of acceptance of ability for admission to a doctoral programme.

Task: the place of your research degree programme in the range available

- Where does your research degree programme fit in terms of the bullet points that outline the kinds of research degree study available in the UK?
- Is it clear to you how your programme is distinctive in these terms and hence what is required of you as a student?

(If it is not clear then you need to read the programme literature again or seek advice from your supervisor – what you need to ascertain is what the award for which you are studying requires of you as a student, e.g. does it mean that you have to engage in a particular kind of research or learn a particular set of research skills and techniques?)

Suggestions for further reading

It might help your understanding of some of these key issues to do with the distinctiveness of research degree study to refer to publications listed in Further Reading: see Section 1 for publications giving the student's perspective and Section 7 for issues of policy at a more global level.

Researching on the one hand and studying on the other

It is arguable that research degree study involves two distinct activities that are not always mutually compatible: researching on the one hand and studying on the other. Indeed, it has sometimes seemed to me as someone who has trained supervisors over a number of years, that supervision of research degree study is sometimes misunderstood as being wholly about supervising the research itself (with what the student learns as a secondary matter) or conversely as being wholly about training the student (with the research findings being subsidiary to, and of lesser importance, than the student's learning). To me both of these interpretations are hard to sustain in the reality of what needs to go on in any research degree context.

I guess my supervisor sees her job as very much training me to be a researcher. She treats me like an apprentice – which is fine by me. She is always talking about how I need to learn research skills and techniques for doing this and that and she keeps on at me to go on courses and to conferences. Sometimes I feel as if what I will eventually submit is taking second place. In a way she doesn't show so much interest in that or at least she isn't as anxious about that as I am. It's me that keeps saying 'but I need to get experiments done for my thesis'. But I am doing them and I guess it will all be all right in the end.

(Second year PhD student studying in bioscience)

As noted above, as a research student you need to learn about research through doing research. To do this successfully you will need to study a whole variety of things, depending on the nature and demands of the research project that develops and within the context of the research degree criteria to which you are working. The one thing that I can say with some certainty is that, inevitably, part of that study will be about how research can be designed and carried out. You may have to learn about the existing state of knowledge in the substantive area within which you have chosen to work, but that will never be enough. To gain a research degree award you will always need to engage with the process of doing research and, with that engagement, comes the challenge of investigation, may come the excitement of discovery but above all will necessarily come some risk.

I think it is important at this stage that I make the point as clearly as I can that, for me at least, real research involves uncertainty and therefore the student who studies about and through researching must be engaged in activity that carries with it that kind of uncertainty. If research is worth doing then its results must be capable of surprising you and your supervisors: clearly certainty of outcome at the beginning of a project would offer no such element of surprise. Of course, as a researcher, you can learn to minimize any risk in that you can design experiments or studies so that they will always tell you something and a well designed research programme will yield findings or outcomes that will suffice to meet the criteria for the award in question. But in all of this, asking research questions is a matter of putting your understandings and ideas on the line and testing them out. This then is the final defining feature of research degree study I wish to highlight. As a research student you need to learn; but you also need to research and therefore you cannot know at the outset just what you will learn at the finish (if indeed there ever is a 'finish'). To return to the dichotomy I set out at the start of this section, research degree study is not a matter of wholly and exclusively researching nor is it a matter of wholly and exclusively studying. It is a matter of learning about research, and about being a researcher, through doing research. The pedagogy is specific because it is arguable that one cannot learn about research in a way that will make one able to operate as an independent researcher without engaging in the object of one's study – that is in researching.

From your perspective as a returning student, I think you need to accept that what research degree study will require of you is that you open your mind to possibilities that you may not have considered before and that you actively seek out the challenge of discovery and in so doing strive to understand the processes, both formal and informal, that shape reasonable ways of discovery that go beyond the immediate (research) task in hand. You might argue that engaging in education is always a matter of 'opening one's mind to possibilities', and I for one would not demure from that position; but research degree study is distinctive in requiring that you create new understandings rather than simply open your mind to the possibility that they might exist.

Suggestions for further reading

See Section 1 of Further Reading for publications that elaborate on the relationship between study and research.

Summary

- You have considered the distinguishing features of research degree study as they relate to you as a student returning to study.
- You have thought about the basic issues surrounding studying about research through doing it.
- You have reflected on the relationship of your research study work with any professional life that you may have.
- You have considered various notions involved in research degree study (notably curriculum, investigation, criticality, self-direction, and prospective outcomes of study).

Conclusion

At root level, research degree study is distinctive from all other forms of academic study because it requires that you learn about how to add to the sum total of understanding through a process of attempting to do just that. This contrasts with the other forms of study where you are required to learn what it is agreed that you will learn. From this crucial distinction flow the various other differences and special features that will be explored in the rest of this book, most notably that a key aim for you is to develop a way of thinking and acting that is characterized by question and typified by investigation. In this latter respect it may help, at this point, for you to re-read and reflect upon the quotation from Nietzsche that opened this chapter; to become a thinker in the way in which he describes may require you to re-evaluate how you treat your own actions as a student and how you interpret and make use of outcomes that appear at first sight to signify only success or failure.

3

Studying for which kind of research degree?

Overview • Introduction • Kinds of research degree study • Levels of research degree award • Notions of 'doctorateness' specifically • Research degree study and the professions • Summary • Conclusion

If we knew what it was we were doing, it would not be called research would it?
Albert Einstein (1875–1955)

Overview

This chapter addresses the different ways in which academia deals with study through research in terms of the various academic awards on offer at research degree level and the implications for you as an individual returning to study in terms of the choices you need to make and the kinds of experiences (of study and of researching) that are likely to follow from your choices, as well as the kinds of award that you may attain ultimately. In this chapter, therefore, you will be asked to:

- consider the different kinds of research degree study, including the various masters, the professional doctorates, the practice-based doctorate and the PhD by published work
- examine the notion of 'doctorateness', including understandings of what it

means to contribute to knowledge and/or to the development of your profession, understandings of originality, as well as 'academic knowledge' versus 'professional knowledge and skill'
- consider the notion of establishing a thesis, developing an argument to support it and subsequently defending it.

Introduction

Having tried to establish in Chapter 2 what is distinctive about research degree study, I now intend to unpick some of the issues relating to both the kinds of research degree study in which you may engage and the levels at which those kinds operate. It may seem to you, especially if you have already chosen both your kind and level of study, that this will not be relevant. However, I would argue that understanding where your form of study fits in the greater scheme of academic study and award may help you to make the most of it and be effective in dealing with the challenges it brings.

In all of this dealing with the pragmatic intricacies of the way universities structure their research training programmes I urge you not to lose sight of the fact that the various differences should not obscure the central point of doing a research degree, which is to learn about what research means and how to go about doing it successfully. All routes have this in common and therefore they all need to grapple with the notion that Einstein comments upon (see quotation at start of the chapter). Einstein makes his point with a characteristic sense of irony – some might suggest with flippancy – but this belies the fact that he is directing our attention to a fundamental aspect of researching. We may think that we know 'what we are doing' by employing research methods that are appropriate to the research question but even here there is a sense in which we cannot know this for sure until we start to see results. More importantly perhaps, Einstein's words may be interpreted as reminding us that research is necessarily about the unknown – and that therefore we, as researchers, have to go through a phase of not knowing. In the context of this chapter, I think you need to recognize that this applies to the research degree study upon which you are embarking as much as it does to any other piece of research activity. Sooner or later doing research means working within the realms of the unknown.

Kinds of research degree study

Disciplinary differences

There are some central features of research degree study that do not, or at least should not, change whatever the discipline you are working within; for example, in my view the doctoral criteria should be constant across disciplines. However, to follow this example, it is also clear that the kinds of evidence that you as a student might bring to bear in your submission to justify your claim to have met those criteria may vary. So, while all doctoral candidates might be expected to make a contribution to knowledge (or, in the case of professional doctorates, to some sub-set of knowledge), the way in which that is achieved is likely to vary from, for example, the visual arts (where such a contribution might be seen as inherent in the student's art works themselves) to the natural sciences (where experimental hypotheses might need to be tested in controlled environments to offer proof of a finding; and the finding in turn might be describable as the contribution). In the UK at least, research degree study can be undertaken in all intellectual disciplines and each will have its own interpretation of what counts as study, data, investigation, analysis and, again, contribution.

In all of this I think it is important that you conceive of your own disciplinary area as being both as alike and as different as all the others; seeing your discipline as the odd one out is likely to lead to an isolationist view and one that is counterproductive to collaborative research ventures and to understanding how your own work may impact on the wider world.

Modes of study

Many UK universities, though not all, allow research degree study in both full-time and part-time modes. There will be no difference between these modes of study in terms of what is expected of students registered in either mode at the point of submission for the award. In short, students registered in either mode will be required to meet the same criteria for the award at the end of their studies. But clearly, there is a big difference in the amount of time that can be committed to your studies depending on whether you are able to devote yourself to your research programme on a full-time basis or not. For this reason most universities who offer a part-time mode of study at research degree level accommodate to this variation in amount of student input to the task by varying the time frames for completion within their regulations. Part-time students may get twice as much time to complete the various phases of study and overall time to completion as those studying full-time. This rather crude pro-rata dealing with deadlines and other aspects of registration can create an illusion of order and compensation but in reality the 'twice as long' notion is not based on anything other than administrative convenience; the notion of engaging in study on a part-time basis covers a range of realities.

Most institutions, however, tend to be understanding about the pressures of life upon their part-time students and use devices such as 'suspension' to address them. Suspension (there are local variations in the terminology used) is when a student applies to stop working on his or her programme temporarily for some reason. If this is agreed by the institution, his or her research degree registration then goes into a kind of suspended state where the clock stops ticking on all time frames within the registration process and importantly, where fees are not paid until the period of suspension comes to an end. You should note that many institutions have strict restrictions on how long periods of suspension may be and how many periods can be applied for by any one student and the kinds of reasons that need to be given to justify them. You should also note that, usually, if your registration is suspended you are not entitled to access the university resources and these include, of course, supervision. If the issue comes up in your own case then you need to read your own institutional regulations carefully and talk to your supervisors and/or any research tutors who are available to you about what is best to do. Usually, the possibilities inherent in mechanisms such as suspension apply equally to both full-time and part-time students.

Suggestions for further reading

There are a number of texts in Section 8 of Further Reading that refer specifically to issues of interest to part-time and to 'mature' students.

The range and levels of research degree awards

The other feature of research degree study where differences apply is that of the varying forms of award for which you may study. I describe the three basic levels of award in the next section; you can study for what may be termed the 'traditional' research degree awards such as MPhil and PhD but also for a professional doctorate (of which there are an ever increasing number) or indeed for a practice-based research degree or one gained through published work (rather than by 'traditional' submission of a dissertation or thesis). I will not dwell on these kinds of award here because they feature in the rest of this chapter and elsewhere in this book. However, I feel it is important to note that, when discussing research degree study, the specific award for which you register and finally submit makes a difference in terms of kind of work that you will engage in and the way in which you are treated in terms of regulatory structures and, perhaps most importantly, how you will be examined. I will try to unpick all of these differences as I go through the various topics of this book.

Levels of research degree award

Broad distinction between levels

I will deal with the detail of the distinction between levels of research degree award by focusing, in the following section, on the criteria that relate to them. But in broad terms the levels of research degree award are realized within the following dimensions:

- The employment of a range of research skills
- Technical competence as a researcher
- The criticality with which published research is reviewed and discussed and with which the candidate's own research programme is conceptualized and carried out
- The originality of the research work in its conception and in any results accruing
- The significance of findings
- The 'publishability' of findings
- The substantive nature of any contribution to knowledge made.

These dimensions are not clear-cut and often examiners will have difficulty in deciding on, for example, level of criticality when it comes to making an award. Similarly, all research degree study should be 'original' in that the student should be undertaking it for the first time. In Table 3.1 on levels of research degree study, I have tried to delineate the way in which achievements in terms of these dimensions can be mapped onto the levels but you should be aware that this is an inexact science and individual examiners and indeed institutions may interpret things differently. I suggest that you use the table as a guide only and interrogate your own institutional regulations to better establish a clear picture for how things are likely to be when your own research work is judged.

Criteria for the various levels of research degree awards

As mentioned, there are levels within the overall notion of research degrees and nominally there are three such levels: doctoral, MPhil and (research) masters. I need to stress once again that local interpretations may apply and you need to check out with your university just what they require of the different levels of award. Indeed, not all universities will offer all three levels and some may treat some awards (perhaps most notably the MPhil) in ways that differ from what I describe below. I am giving the generality and you must recognize that, in the UK at least, this will always be tempered by local differences. While all universities in the UK will be operating within the National Framework for academic awards (the Framework for Higher Education Qualifications (FHEQ), details can be found on the Quality Assurance Agency (QAA) website: http://www.qaa.ac.uk/academicinfrastructure/FHEQ/EWNI/default.asp#framework, accessed 5 August 2008), nevertheless different interpretations will apply and different usages made of the various award titles (for example, as already noted, some universities make very little, if any, use of professional doctoral titles while others offer a plethora – and further, a minority of UK universities refer to all professional doctorates, of whatever discipline/profession, with the generic title of DProf).

In Table 3.1 I have set out the nature of the gradation between levels. Again, I stress that this should be used as a guide only. A room full of academics could most probably spend some considerable time and energy in disputing and/or clarifying the distinctions that I make in these levels. You need to use Table 3.1 as a way to explore the situation in your institution.

Table 3.1 Levels of research degree study

In this table I have tried to set out the way in which the criteria for the levels of research degree award differ. You will notice that in my suggestions the doctoral level subsumes all of the criteria in the lower levels. For convenience in each level I have italicized what is additional to the level below. Essentially therefore all that is required of a research masters will be required at the higher levels but there will be additional requirements; similarly all that is required of an MPhil will be required of a doctorate and in addition those things that are italicized will be needed.

Doctoral level (e.g. PhD, DPhil) typically involves:
- substantial programme of individual research
- sustained exercise of independent critical powers including the ability to use research outcomes to guide the development of the research programme
- *significant, original contribution to knowledge*
- thesis presented and defended in a scholarly manner
- *containing material worthy of peer-reviewed publication*
- technical competence in the chosen field
- an appreciation of the context and significance of the thesis

Master of Philosophy level (MPhil) typically involves:
- a *substantial* programme of individual research
- *sustained* exercise of independent critical powers *including the ability to use research outcomes to guide the development of the research programme*
- thesis presented and defended in a lucid and scholarly manner
- technical competence in the chosen field
- *appreciation of the context and significance of the thesis*

Research Masters level (e.g. MRes (Masters in Research); MA/MSc (Masters by Research)) typically involves:
- a programme of individual research
- exercise of independent critical powers (with a particular emphasis on research methodology)
- thesis presented and defended in a lucid and scholarly manner
- technical competence in the chosen field

Task: analysing standard of award

Find, within your university's regulations or student handbook, the criteria for the award that is your intended goal and note how it compares and/or contrasts with those suggested in Table 3.1.

- Where there are differences, are they of substance or merely matters of wording?
- What are the implications of what you have found in the regulations for your own research study?

All research degrees involve, *inter alia*, learning about research through doing research. You will be assessed on what you have learnt about researching and how independently you have shown that you can operate as a researcher. What Table 3.1 shows is how the need to be able to guide the development of future research programmes in an independent and self-sustaining way is ratcheted up as candidates move up through the levels of research degree award. You need to be aware of this whatever level you are operating at, and whether or not you intend to move up through the levels. It is perhaps worth noting here that this latter 'moving up' is very often a feature of research degree study, with the levels I have described often being mapped imprecisely onto phases of research programmes. I use the term 'imprecisely' because research programmes and findings and subsequent programmes that build on earlier ones are notoriously hard to separate out in phases of study that can be mapped with real precision onto regulatory time frames. Nevertheless, in many universities within the UK students can register at one level, demonstrate their capability at that level and then progress (or upgrade or transfer) to the next level. In this way research degree study can be seen as linear in terms of the student experience though this is not universal and, because of the nature of research, is often imprecise.

Suggestions for further reading

Section 7 of Further Reading contains publications that may be of interest if you want to explore national understandings of the levels of research degree study and the criteria for the awards.

Notions of 'doctorateness' specifically

Making a contribution

Many university regulations will refer to a 'contribution to knowledge' when setting out criteria for the doctorate (again I refer to other levels below), others will refer to understanding or to learning and some may include a contribution to the skills needed for particular intellectual tasks or procedures. I think what I need to indicate here is that, as a general rule, the notion of the kind of contribution that needs to be made is broader than any narrow interpretation of knowledge itself as a collection of facts and figures. In short, there are variations across the disciplines and across kinds of doctorate in terms of what counts as a valid contribution. I think for you as a student developing or working through a programme of study you need to focus on the word 'contribution' in the first instance. You need to reflect upon what would count within your discipline(s) as a contribution to the understandings of those working within that discipline(s). I give some possibilities below, not in an attempt to cover all options but rather to indicate the kinds of ways in which an intellectual contribution might be made to various disciplines.

- *Factual knowledge*: your contribution might be in making known some aspect of knowledge whereby a 'new thing' is known about some aspect of the world (or indeed beyond the world).
- *Processes and procedures*: your contribution might relate to processes or procedures. So, for example, it might be a procedure for undertaking further, safe, experimentation on particular, volatile, chemicals; it might be a way of predicting patterns within sections of financial markets from given data sets; it might be a new way of analysing historical data to reveal trends.
- *New ways of interpreting*: your contribution might be realized in terms of new ways of interpreting existing phenomena be they natural, artificial or artistic (not claiming these to be mutually exclusive of course).
- *Skills*: your contribution might relate to an increasing understanding of specific skills such that those who need to employ those skills are made more effective. For example, it may be that you contribute to an increased awareness of the skills needed by paramedics in instances where patients have suspected heart failure or indeed that you contribute to an understanding of new ways of training and/or assessing those skills.

Another way of looking at the issue of contribution is to say that what is required at research degree level (and at doctoral level specifically – see the section where other research degree levels are delineated) is that experts within your chosen intellectual field learn something for themselves from reading your submission and from your defence of it. At the end of your studies you have to contribute to their understanding of your chosen aspects of the world or indeed their appreciation of those aspects. In short, the small panel of experts chosen to be your examiners have to be persuaded that you have contributed to their understanding, that having read your work and questioned you on it they now know something, or appreciate something, that they did not know or appreciate before.

Understandings of originality at doctoral level

I have already noted in this chapter that originality is a hard concept to pin down when it comes to differentiating levels of research degree study. Certainly, one might legitimately expect all work at research degree level to be original in that it should be research undertaken by the student for the first time. Yet you will have noticed that I excluded it from Table 3.1 (Levels of research degree study) at both levels below that of doctorate. This is because one needs to draw a distinction between on the one hand doing research that is original in that you as the student are doing a specific research study for the first time and on the other hand the doing of a piece of research in such a way as to lead to an original contribution to knowledge. The former will not necessarily lead to the latter; that is, one might work on something in an original way but not necessarily produce an understanding of knowledge that is new.

It is important here to state that the intellectual position that you adopt as a result of your studies (see the section on 'thesis' below) is where your originality should be located.

Having said this I think it is worth noting that, for me at least, it is possible to interpret originality in fairly liberal terms. I am not suggesting above that something has to be wholly new to be counted as original. Indeed, one might argue that new ideas are always based on old understandings ('there is nothing original under the sun') and what is being asked for at doctoral level in this respect may therefore be a reshaping of old understandings or a different perspective on a given phenomenon or a repositioning of the way in which questions need to be asked of future phenomena. In my view, you need to be acutely aware of what is required by way of originality but not overawed by the prospect of achieving it in your own research work. Lots of doctorates are awarded each year and your work *can* lead to you being among that number.

Research degree study and the professions

Distinctive notions of 'contribution' within professional doctorate awards

---

Tasks: contribution to knowledge?
- What might count as a 'significant original contribution' to knowledge within your discipline or profession?
- Refer to the university criteria for the award of the degree you are considering or embarking upon and note down what you have to demonstrate in order to gain the award, i.e. just what is it that you have to do to get the degree you are seeking?

The criteria say that I have to undertake a 'substantial programme of individual research'; it has to involve the 'sustained exercise of independent critical powers'; I have to be able to use research outcomes to 'guide the development of my research programme'. I guess this means I have to know what results mean in terms of developing my own research ideas. Finally, it has to lead to a 'significant original contribution to professional practice and/or the enterprise(s) in which the programme is carried out'. The last bit strikes me as odd wording but seems to allow something a bit more specific than the 'contribution to professional practice' notion, so I guess I am happy with that. It was actually quite useful to read the words with some care because frankly I had not done that before. I had just wanted to get on to the programme and then to get started on some investigation. I have now begun to think about where all this is leading me.

(First year EngD student)

I have already mentioned professional areas in which contributions might be made. But the growth in professional doctorate awards demands that I devote a section to what is required within these degrees. There is talk in the literature about so-called 'academic knowledge' versus 'professional knowledge' often with attendant arguments suggesting that both need to be valued. Personally I find these arguments a little redundant. To me there is knowledge, and it may or may not be located within a profession; it may be knowledge that is generated within, and for the benefit of, a given profession (and ultimately its clients) or it may be knowledge that is generated in the world at large and applied within a profession. Location and generation may not matter for our purposes here; it seems to me that what does matter is that where knowledge, skills or indeed intellectually based processes and procedures, make a specific contribution to a particular profession – then they can be used legitimately as part of a claim for a professional doctoral award.

I should also note here however that such a contribution might well be submitted successfully for a PhD award (i.e. rather than, for example, an EngD or an EdD). I am making the point here that professional doctorates do not have exclusivity when it comes to the use of so-called 'professional knowledge' as the basis for academic awards. For example, within many institutions in the UK a PhD student might submit for his or her award based on a project looking at reading styles of children from different subcultural groups and subsequent implications for pedagogy; yet clearly this topic is also one that might be pursued by a candidate for a Doctor in Education award (EdD). The matter then of what award is applied for in the submission is a matter that is decided by the local (i.e. institutional) constraints of the kinds of awards available; some UK universities simply do not offer EdD programmes and hence awards yet a candidate may still study within the discipline of Education for an award (typically PhD). I use the EdD here as an example but I suggest that the same applies across all professional doctorates.

Of course, I am not saying here that there is no difference between the PhD on the one hand and the range of professional doctorates on the other. Clearly, the processes through which a candidate may study, the kinds of input from staff that can be expected and, importantly, the kinds of group or cohort support available may be quite distinctive within a professional doctorate setting. But I would argue that the kind of contribution made is a matter of location rather than real substance. I should add that this view is my own and you will find some academics who do not subscribe to it and who see more profound differences between the PhD and professional doctorates. What you need to do as a student is look at the criteria for the award as they apply in your chosen university and compare and contrast those for the different awards. In my own view there should be no difference in doctoral *standard* between awards; teaching and learning processes that lead to the award may be very different but 'kind of contribution made' should have a sense of parity – after all, the professional doctorate awards and indeed the PhD by published work are all at doctoral level. All successful candidates may be called 'Doctor' and all should be capable of operating at a doctoral level.

I should also note here that the UK is fairly idiosyncratic in terms of the number of professional doctorate awards on offer within its universities. Many other countries have no comparable named awards (and hence many academics from overseas will express lack of understanding of them), i.e. countries beyond the UK's borders may have the PhD but no other named awards at doctoral level.

Suggestions for further reading

Section 7 of Further Reading contains publications that may be of interest if you want to explore some of the policy and practice issues relating to professional doctorates. Some of the more general issues relating to higher education can be found in Section 11.

Summary

- You have thought about how academia deals with study through research in terms of its various awards and the implications for you as an individual returning to study.
- You have considered what it means to contribute to knowledge and/or to the development of your profession.
- You have contemplated different understandings of originality.
- You have been introduced to the notion of establishing a thesis, developing an argument to support it and subsequently defending it.

Conclusion

Different kinds of research degree award require of you as a student different approaches to both research and to learning about research. Yet despite all the differences between the different kinds and levels of award that have been considered in this chapter there are common themes. Your research degree programme will necessarily require that you learn about research by reading about it and discussing it with others and, crucially, through doing it. Your programme will enable you to come to an adequate understanding of the art and the science of doing research. At the end of your studies you should be in a position to understand better how previously published research has impacted upon the world (or at least the part of the world that is the focus of your interest) and how best to design, implement, analyse and use your own research not just in the immediate but also in future, ever changing scenarios and according to new pressures and motivations. Doing a research degree is designed to make you into a researcher and that necessarily involves challenging the known and investigating the unknown.

To return to the quotation from Einstein with which I opened this chapter, it must be that to be called research an activity has to have something to do with not knowing, and therefore learning about research is essentially a matter of coming to understand how you can approach the unknown with a reasonable chance of investigating it effectively. You may feel uncomfortable with the idea of 'not knowing what you are doing' (to paraphrase Einstein) but, as I will discuss in later chapters, periods of discomfort may be essential to your growth as a researcher.

4

Thinking and learning

Overview • Introduction • The personal dimension to learning • The need for critical thinking • A place for originality and creativity • Reflection • Summary • Conclusion

> *To be conscious that you are ignorant is a great step to knowledge.*
> Benjamin Disraeli (1804–1881),
> *Sybil, or the Two Nations*, Book 1 (1845)

Overview

This chapter discusses the essentials of effective thinking and learning that underpin the approach taken throughout this book. In this chapter, therefore, you will be asked to:

- examine the place of critical thinking in the whole process of returning to study successfully
- consider making your own learning a point of focus in your studying and researching (it will be suggested that by so doing you will be able to improve your abilities as a learner and researcher, in a continuing sense, as well as make the learning of particular material more efficient and the carrying out of particular research projects more effective)
- explore the personal dimension to learning as well as the need for critical thinking in the way in which you operate in the workplace (where appropriate), particularly in the way in which you can use research investigations

and the research findings of others to enhance your own professional practice (again, where appropriate)

- consider the implications of all this for your academic study and in so doing unpick the place for originality and creativity in the interface between professional practice, researching and studying for an academic award
- contemplate the place of reflection in relation to the above.

Introduction

As you read this chapter you will be reflecting on your own style as a learner and researcher and thinking about the need to engage with learning and researching at an evaluative level; that is to make appropriate value judgements about new knowledge and skills. My own view is that key to your progress as a thinker and a learner about research is the notion of reflection, which is acknowledged obliquely by Disraeli in the quotation above: the implication being that you need to think constructively about the limits of your knowledge and the boundaries of your professional skills and the way in which researching can extend those limits and push back those boundaries.

The personal dimension to learning

Being conscious of ignorance

From my perspective, someone who returns to study as a research degree student wanting to demonstrate that something they already believe to be the case, often from their own extensive experience in their professional or non-professional life, is in fact 'the case' is in danger of ploughing a sterile intellectual furrow. Certainly, it is possible to enter a research degree programme wanting to test out, for example, something that you have come to believe is good, effective professional practice; but you have to be prepared to find out that this is not the case. Indeed, you might be better to set out to try to prove yourself wrong – then failure to do so might give your original 'theory' some credence. While I am using the notion of a kind of null-hypothesizing here I am not restricting my comments to scientific design. It seems to me that there is an important distinction that you as a returning student need to recognize. While you might want to test out ideas in a research degree programme, you would be ill-advised to merely want to demonstrate to others what you already think you know. The former is appropriate as a basis for research degree study – while the latter is not; as Mark Twain would have it, 'It is wiser to find out than to suppose'.

A sense of inquiry and an interest in the challenge of changing the way things are, and the way you are yourself, are important parts of any process of effective learning. The implication of Disraeli's words ('To be conscious that you are ignorant is a great step to knowledge') is that awareness that one does not know is prerequisite to coming to know about something. As a returning student you need to recognize that, despite previous learning and any professional experience you may have, there remain things that you can learn profitably about both your work and about yourself as a learner, and that this is particularly pertinent at research degree level. I think that there is a need for you to conceive of your approaching a research degree programme as an opportunity for self-improvement and self-fulfilment at a more fundamental level than the mere accumulation of more knowledge and skill.

Of course Disraeli's words only take us so far. Certainly, it is important to be conscious that there are things about your work outside of academia that you still need to learn but it is also necessary to come to an understanding of how you have learnt what you have so far and how you are continually learning new material and new skills. Research is not something that is engaged in only by professional researchers doing defined research projects using formally approved methods. It is a way of thinking and behaving that is present in much of what we as human beings do from childhood onwards. Of course, doing research degree study will enable you to rationalize and properly describe and understand some of these naturalistic ways of investigating but you would be unwise to reify research to a point where it attains some unreachable status in your mind. You need to recognize where in your existing professional and personal lives you already, for example, investigate, seek out alternatives, test out truths and find ways of explaining phenomena.

Task: recognizing existing research activity
- Note down instances where you employ investigative techniques – however primitive or everyday they may seem – in your professional or personal life.
- What 'research skills' do these instances indicate that you already have (even if in incipient form)?

I suppose I use what might be called investigative techniques when I diagnose a patient's problem. I ask questions, I take a look, I prod a bit and if necessary I take an X-ray to take, effectively, a look inside. Sometimes I open up the tooth to see what is going on. Sometimes I can work it out from the patient's description, sometimes I need more evidence. I would hardly call this researching but investigating – yes. Actually, when I think about it, I guess I do problem solving each and every day and I am in fact pretty systematic in how I move from a patient coming in with a painful tooth to a diagnosis and then to a course of treatment.

(Dental surgeon enrolled on an MD programme)

Recognition of possibilities, your own potential and your individual approach to learning

It may be some years since you undertook sustained study and therefore studying, often in addition to a heavy workload, may seem an unfamiliar and forbidding challenge. It is important however to recognize that your return to study can be done successfully (the evidence is probably all around you) and that you already possess the kinds of skills that can be harnessed to enable you to work effectively in the new (research degree) domain. It may be a matter of taking a fresh look at the kinds of skills you already use that may be applicable to, or adaptable for, learning in the context of renewed academic study. You need to unravel for yourself the strategies that are most effective for you. It is perhaps worth stating the obvious here: learning is very much an individual business. Each of us thinks and learns in different ways, some of which may seem superficial but many of which are fundamental. For example, the way in which individuals are able to use the visual representation of material in their learning will vary considerably; diagrams, plans and illustrations will have different value across any range of students. For example, one of the students (a therapist) who commented on some of the ideas in this book described the way in which she used a flowchart:

> To get a structure about a problem, to find my orientation, I use a flowchart. When I prepare an exam or presentation I take key words and make it all fit on one side of A4. I make a path that has smaller paths leading off it. I use it with clients as well to give them another way of working.

I am not, here, advocating the use of flowcharts in particular but rather I am using this as an example of the kind of reflection on your own learning preferences and style that you need to engage in – a topic which is pursued in the next section.

Suggestions for further reading

If you are interested in issues relating to your own learning, you may wish to refer to Section 8 of Further Reading, which contains some relevant publications.

The need for critical thinking

You will already have got the message that, as far as I am concerned, research degree study is about improving the mind as much as it is about learning particular things and gaining specific research skills. What I want to argue for in this section is that there should be an inevitable symbiosis between your work outside of academia and your return to study in terms of your developing critical thinking abilities. If you are working in a professional context, your professional work may require that you do more than react to events; you will be reflective about what you do and the decisions that you make and you engage in a kind of decision making that is characterized by its critical qualities.

Task: your existing critical thinking behaviours

- What aspects of your work or life outside of your academic studies require you to reflect critically?
- Can you determine examples where your reflections are particularly studied and more deliberate?
- How might the kinds of abilities you have exhibited in these examples be brought to bear on your research degree work?

I guess that when I am training other physiotherapists I deliberately slow down my decision making about a particular 'case' so that they can see how I work out condition, prognosis and treatment.

(Physiotherapist registered for a DNurse)

At drafting stage I let things flow a bit, but when I come to set things down for a presentation to a potential client then, at that stage, I start to check everything out and test my ideas in more detail against the usual checks and balances.

(Student registered for a doctorate in architecture and design)

Advanced (research degree) study requires critical thought and you give evidence of that thought in the way in which you present your ideas, be that in oral or written form. Further, for those within the professions, it is likely that if your programme of study focuses in part or in whole on professional issues then it will involve critical reflection on your professional practice. There is then a coming together of professional and academic work under the umbrella of 'critical thinking'.

What counts as critical thinking

Critical thinking is a term which is widely used and occasionally abused in various parts of the literature. In this chapter it is used to describe a kind of thought processing which is more than routine and non-directed and which reaches levels of clarity and purposefulness that enable you to unravel research problems which are within your range of knowledge and skills. 'Range' is inserted at the end of this working definition because it is important to recognize that critical thinking is, in one sense at least, independent of levels of knowledge and skill. You may operate in a mode of critical thought at your current level of knowledge and skill whatever that may be. Of course, you may not reach a 'correct' conclusion in this sense but that becomes less significant (in the academic setting if not in the real world) than the fact that you are engaged in a critical way.

It might be helpful therefore if you can separate out your understanding of your ability to think from your knowledge of things and your set of acquired practical skills. This is a rather artificial exercise and is not to suggest that knowledge and practical skills are unimportant, or less important than your ability to think, but simply to recognize that they need to take their place in the whole of your intellectual profile. It would be deceptive to conceive of your return to study at research degree level as a matter of gaining in knowledge without recognizing the corresponding gain in thinking ability that is required. Research degree study can be distinguished from other forms of university level work, as noted in previous chapters, in that it requires that the successful candidate demonstrates an ability to engage critically with the boundaries of knowledge and with their extension rather than simply being concerned with existing knowledge and understanding. To repeat a perhaps mundane example, in doctoral examinations it is usual for candidates to take a copy of their thesis into the examination with them. The questioning that ensues does not require you to remember facts (from within the thesis) but rather to engage critically with the ideas it expounds and the processes and procedures that led you to set out your thesis in the way in which you have.

Critical thinking in the world beyond university study

To think critically means more than simply to be negative about something. Certainly, it involves finding fault. But critical thinking is a matter of finding fault with argument, with the basis upon which evidence is cited and the reasonableness of conclusions reached. If you work within a professional context then it is probably the case that in much of your working life these things are implied. Colleagues may not set out their arguments, the bases for their acceptance of evidence and so on, for your convenience; all of these things may remain implicit. Critical thinking therefore requires a construction on your part of how things have come to be as well as an analysis of what people say or do. When you have constructed in this way, for example, the history of a medical diagnosis that is under question then you can begin to analyse efficacy and begin to hypothesize about prognosis etc. My point in rehearsing all of these things here is to stress the link with research degree study where you are required to analyse what is written in the literature, what is claimed from empirical investigations and what the possibilities are for your own contributing studies, using in all of this the accepted methodologies (of both critiquing and investigating) within your discipline. I suggest therefore that it may be helpful if you conceive of critical thinking in the academic arena as an extension of what you already practise (perhaps unknowingly) in your professional or working life.

Task: critical thinking in the work context

Can you cite an example from your working context which picks up on some aspect of non-critical thinking, for example:

- where individuals reach conclusions without considering all of the relevant features of the situation
- where justifications for decisions reached fail to acknowledge all of the factors involved
- where the implications of decisions are not thought through before implementation?

If so, try to write down where the process of critical thought has broken down – and where, possible identify why that should have been so.

Non-critical thinking – when a professional doesn't see the need to have the background information about the client; for example a client may have challenging behaviour and the professional tries to find a way of reducing this behaviour without finding its cause.

(Psychologist registered for a DClinPsy)

When the government makes efforts to 'raise standards' in schools by, in part, increasing testing without realizing that continual assessment can be a distraction rather than an advantage for children's actual learning.

(Primary school teacher registered for an EdD)

When the [engineering] resolution refers to a range of conditions within the bounds of high to low without recognizing – and addressing – the possibility of the 'extreme'.

(Engineer working for a water company and registered for an engineering doctorate (EngD))

Analysing problem-solving protocols

My contention here is that you can improve your capabilities as a problem solver through a process of analysis of your own problem-solving style and of the features inherent within the tasks that you face. The mechanical engineer facing a malfunctioning engine follows a problem-solving procedure, typically beginning with some hypotheses based on the kind of malfunction that is apparent. Similarly, that same engineer might set about tackling a research project by following a problem-solving procedure; perhaps beginning by trying to make clear to himself or herself just what the project brief requires and within what constraints the 'resolution' is to be delivered (e.g. does the project require an illustration of an approach or the justification of a specific solution to a stated problem). The difference between the workplace and the academic task is, of course, that the former may be more defined and practised than the latter. But I suggest that, for you as a professional returning to research degree study, analysing how you go about solving problems in either one context or the other is likely to be profitable and, again, profit in one domain is likely to feed into the other.

A defining feature of your working practice or academic discipline might be that it requires you to follow certain general heuristics ('rule of thumb' procedures that are likely to set you in the direction of a correct response to the problem situation with which you are faced) or a specific algorithm (a procedure that will necessarily yield a correct solution if followed exactly). Professions and disciplines operate on particular ways of knowing, investigating and responding within problem scenario. For example, a natural scientist may operate on an understanding of a set of fairly immutable laws of nature whereas a social scientist may need to balance probabilities based on an understanding of the way in which the dynamics of social groups within wider cultural contexts suggest likely outcomes of any set of given variables. Similarly, the natural scientist may have commonly accepted investigative procedures that act as a template for various ways of 'finding out' (e.g. involving experimental design that includes the controlling of some variables) while the social scientist may employ quite different approaches to investigation (e.g. using case studies to develop a narrative that better describes the workings of the social groups under study). It may help you to begin to unravel the way in which arguments and procedures are constructed in your area if you can set out a kind of protocol in which you 'think aloud' through a process of problem solving that is typical within your working routines (e.g. deciding on the cause of sudden distress in a premature baby who had previously been settled).

Representation of problems

Table 4.1 sets out some different ways of representing whatever workplace based or academic problem faces you. These alternatives may help to provoke

Table 4.1 Representing problems

Ways of representing	Examples of occasions for use	Possible advantages
Write down in words or figures	Where the presentation of the problem is oral	Saves you the effort of trying to hold the problem state in your head
Restate in your own words	Where the presentation is convoluted or deliberately opaque or ambiguous	Helps you to see what you think you are trying to do – particularly useful in a group problem-solving context where different perceptions of the nature of the question may be helpful
Draw a graph	Where the problem is spatial or involves relationships that change over time	Can present all of the information at one time; can simplify
Draw a diagram	Where the problem relates to a process, or a set of relationships or the development of concepts	Can show how a process fits together or relationships become operative
Create a hierarchy (sometimes referred to as a tree diagram)	Where there are various possible outcomes or different, but equally feasible, routes to a solution	Can help to unravel complex relationships; can indicate how one thing follows from another etc.
Create a matrix	Where there are various combinations of results	Can help to unravel the relationships between categories

you to think about the way in which you first approach a problem-solving task. Of course, Table 4.1 is intended as a guide only, clearly there is considerable overlap between kinds of representation and examples of usage and benefit.

Very often the first thing you have to do in researching is to familiarize yourself with the problem state or the issue and its particular make-up. Thinking about how to represent such things should enable you to begin to think about how to manipulate elements of them in order to better understand them and so begin to find effective ways of resolving, addressing or describing them. For example, it may be that you need to focus on just what it is that makes a chosen problem difficult to resolve simply by asking 'What *is* the problem exactly?' You may need to consider just what it is about the issue in hand that attracts you to it (i.e. what makes it an issue worth considering in the context of research degree study) simply by asking 'Why does this issue arise and why is it of importance?' On the other hand it may be that you need to unravel the overt and covert aspects of the way the research issue presents itself: for example, the paramedic faced with the 'brave' accident victim claiming to need low priority and who displays little visual evidence of injury needs to consider the possibilities of the effects of shock, the likelihood of internal injury in terms of the nature of the accident. In such a situation where all may not be as seems on the surface, what are the bases upon which the paramedic makes decisions, is there commonality in these bases, does any commonality that does exist have implications for ways of training future paramedics and/or establishing treatment protocols? Establishing what is a reasonable research question (and, in this case, one with some kind of professional 'pay-off') is a necessary precursor to deciding on an investigative method(s). You need therefore to find ways of representing the problem or issue (and hence analysing it) before you start to try to investigate it.

If part of the difficulty of the problem or issue that you face is in its lack of definition then clarification may have to be your starting point. Lack of definition requires that you restate the goal in different forms: for example achieving an 'appropriate placement' within social services provision for an adult with learning difficulties might be interpreted as adapting the person's current environment rather than seeking out a new placement, designing more effective components within a combustion engine may require that you redefine what might count as 'efficiency'.

Strategies for solving problems

There is not space in this book to describe adequately all of the kinds of problem-solving strategies that might be available to you in the course of your research study. However, I can note some approaches if only to give an indication of the kinds of ideas that may improve the way in which you go about solving the variety of problems that you will encounter in your return to research degree study. I have chosen to discuss, as contrasting examples from among the range of approaches, the use of means-ends analysis, brainstorming and analogy.

Means-ends analysis

A means-ends analysis will allow you to define research sub-goals that, when achieved, should enable you to progress from the posing of a research question to the main research goal. It is a matter of analysing the problem or issue that you face in terms of what means are required to get you to the 'end', to the desired solution. In terms of research study related to the workplace it may be that in investigating, for example, how clients are treated at the first point of contact, you first need to look at the reasons and circumstances that lead up to that point (i.e. what happens between server and client in this situation is not just a function of the contact but of the reasons for that contact) before you can make progress towards a defining of the precise research question itself and then the most effective method(s) needed to pursue that question.

It may be possible, of course, to determine the means by working back from the end; that is, it may be that you can work backwards from the research goal to your present questioning state. For example, if the research problem or issue relates to an unsatisfactory by-product in a particular process of food production then it may be necessary to work out how it comes about that the by-product is caused before you can work out what can be done about the whole of the production process.

Brainstorming

Brainstorming is when you set down on paper as many ideas relating to a research theme, or possible solutions to a research problem, as you can in a random and spontaneous way. Some dismiss this technique as merely a chance to say or write down anything that comes into the head without having to justify or explain it and suggest that it offers little that is productive, while others see it as a useful way to generate ideas without being restricted by artificial boundaries. Most commonly used as a group activity it can, however, be used on an individual basis. In my own experience it carries with it the possible advantage of freeing students from the kind of psychological constraints that sometimes impede research problem solving. If you feel locked into a particular kind of solution or 'accepted' way of proceeding then letting your mind generate ideas in an unfettered way can be liberating. It is, however, likely to be only the first stage in a research process. If you use a brainstorming technique, for example to generate ideas about how to solve a problem of access to facilities for a particular client group, then you will still need to refine your original list of ideas, perhaps into categories (e.g. those dealing with practical solutions of how to get people to the 'product', those which change the nature of the 'product' so as to make it more accessible to the people and so on) and then into some kind of rank order of practicality, cost, acceptability by the client group etc.

Analogy

Using analogy in research is a matter of going through a process of reasoning by using parallel cases. In the workplace you may have tried to explain something complex to a client who has no specialist knowledge and found yourself resorting to 'it's like . . .' and then using an analogy which relates the technical to the everyday experience of that client, for example 'when the water rises as you get into the bath' or 'the layers of an onion'. Just as analogy is useful in explaining complex material to others so it can be a useful device in helping you to interpret a research problem state facing you. I have found with my own students that encouraging them to develop an analogy for themselves allows them to recast a complex problem which appears to be outside of their range of experience into a form with which they are familiar and they are then able to begin to manipulate ideas. My suggestion here is that you may be able to use analogy as an approach to research problem solving, for example you might think of the physical elements of an engineering problem as a group of people, who reject and accept each other, and thus come to a clearer understanding of the dynamic structures within the particular problem state (and how they may be manipulated).

Suggestions for further reading

For publications that refer to critical thinking in general and to ways of learning how to think critically in particular, please refer to Section 9 of Further Reading.

A place for originality and creativity

You might think that originality and creativity belong in the 'arts' areas and have little to do with other areas of academic study and professional life. But I think this would be a misguided view. In many cases in higher education there will be tasks which are open-ended and where outcomes are not clearly defined in advance of the undertaking of the work. In research degree study this is more likely to be the rule than the exception. 'Originality' is a *sine qua non* of research study – certainly at doctoral level. Where at taught degree level it is sometimes the student who offers an original interpretation of a set question who receives the higher grade, at research degree level such originality is required if you are to be successful. Similarly, the very nature of much professional work that demands a doctoral level qualification requires creative solutions to be found to everyday problems, often at the interface between disciplines or professional groups. Doctoral workers are expected to be the ones in the workplace who come up with the creative solution to problems and hence professional doctorates are in the business of inculcating such skills in their students.

In your research degree study you are likely to need to think divergently as well as convergently; that is to think around and beyond problems as well as to focus on a research solution in the immediate. You are likely to need to express sensitivity to issues and to use imagination to predict outcomes. Also, I hope you will find that there is a place for risk-taking as already mentioned. Indeed, as I have already argued I would suggest that at the sharp edge of research inquiry a project without any kind of intellectual risk attached is unlikely to prove profitable. Creativity may be hard to identify and to judge but this does not deny its existence or lessen its value.

Reflection: a place for creativity?

Is there a place for creativity in your workplace outside of academia?

If there is, then:

- How is it manifest?
- How is it evaluated by you (if at all)?
- How is it judged by others?

People think engineering is a matter of working systematically to achieve set goals but in fact solving engineering problems is a very creative business – though I guess our creativity is not really evaluated as such – but the results are.

(Engineer registered for an engineering doctorate (EngD))

The highest praise my partner has heaped upon me is to say that I have completed some of the most imaginative bridgework he has ever seen.

(Dental surgeon registered for a medical doctorate (MD))

Suggestion for further reading

For an interesting take on creative action see Parnes et al. (1977) in Section 9 of Further Reading.

Reflection

Reflection as a way to effective learning

It is seductive to think that if only one could learn particular research techniques then researching would become easier. In reality it is likely that effective research practice has more to do with awareness and understanding of the purposes and processes of researching than with techniques or mechanical skills. I know that all the research students I meet who are re-entering the world of study *can* learn about research, but I am also aware that those who will become the more effective learners about research are those who find ways of reflecting on their own learning about research and therefore give themselves opportunities to gain control over that learning and hence ultimately over their own proactive researching.

Evaluative appraisal

The defining feature of reflection, which distinguishes it from mere recall, is that it contains some evaluation of what has happened. A necessary feature of effective learning about research for you, therefore, is that it involves you in an ongoing process of evaluating what is being learnt in terms of its effect on your wider knowledge and ability to understand issues – failure to engage with learning about research in this evaluative way is likely to lead to a restricted understanding and in turn a lessening in the likelihood that you will be able to design and carry out worthwhile and productive research studies on your own in a sustained way following your university programme of studies.

You may doubt this and cite examples from your own experience where learning by rote (i.e. without any evaluative appraisal) has been effective for you and hence you might argue that at least some things about researching may be learnt in a non-critical way. But if you think carefully about the effects of such rote learning then you may recognize that while you can learn information by rote and without any evaluative reflection, that learning is always likely to be limited. First, there are limits to how much you can learn in this way, and second, recall of that information is constrained by the need for the appropriate cues. As a research student you need to be able to think flexibly and in a self-initiated way, you cannot afford to be dependent on any particular set of cues. I am suggesting here that you might try to engage with new learning about research at a personal level, i.e. 'How does this affect *me* as a learner about research and the way in which *I* understand the world and can understand it better through research?' Notions that learning about research and solving problems through research require objectivity are misleading. It is subjectivity that denotes learning as being of the human kind and which takes it out of the realms of what, for example, a computer can 'learn'.

Making use of an active listener

It may well be that, in your return to research degree study, more so than to other forms of study, there is an important role to be played by someone operating as an active listener; that is, listening and reflecting back to you what you appear to be saying and proposing to do in your research so that greater clarity can be achieved. It can be the case that students working in isolation have difficulty in developing their ideas if they do not have some way of making their views known to another and getting constructive feedback. It has to be noted that isolation has been one of the key negative features of doctoral study in the UK that has driven the recent reforms of the Quality Assurance Agency (QAA) in the form for example of the revised Code of Practice (see the QAA website for details) and is partially the source of the increased focus upon so-called 'generic training courses' for research students as well as the general increase in support from supervisors (who are now quite likely to have been formally trained).

Of course the kind of dialogue noted at the start of this section can be achieved in the process of handing in drafts of research write-ups and receiving back comments, but that process inevitably involves delay and does not always allow a debate of the kind that is envisaged here. Essential though written feedback is, it is also the case that one way or another you need to try to make use of someone who can listen to what you say about your research and engage with you in a meaningful discussion about it.

Summary

- You have been introduced to the ideas which underpin this book and the benefits of an active and evaluative approach to learning about research have been highlighted.
- You have been encouraged to think of strategies for adopting a critical, reflective approach in your research work. These strategies may or may not involve others and will operate at different levels of formality. As in any case of returning to study at university, but particularly at research degree level, the choice of strategies and their deployment is necessarily and properly yours.

Conclusion

If, in a self-evaluative sense, you can say that you have recognized things in the world that you do not fully understand and recognized things about yourself as a learner about research, then you can reassure yourself that you have taken the step recommended by Disraeli in the quote at the beginning of this chapter, that is towards knowledge both of things and of yourself (in this case as a researcher). Alongside this self-awareness needs to be a determination to develop critical faculties about all aspects of research as well as to accumulate knowledge; as Confucius is reputed to have noted: 'Learning without thought is labour lost; thought without learning is perilous'.

5

Working and communicating with others

> *I do then with my friends as I do with my books. I would have them where I can find them, but I seldom use them.*
>
> Ralph Waldo Emerson (1803–1882),
> 'Friendship', in *Essays: First Series* (1841)

Overview

Research rarely occurs in a social vacuum and this chapter addresses the ways in which you can make use of others in your work and can, in turn, learn to contribute to the intellectual arena within which your research programme takes place. In this chapter, therefore, you will be asked to:

- consider ways of working effectively with your peers and with supervisors both at university (e.g. in group, research-based projects) and within any relevant professional work setting (e.g. in research groups or in groups influenced by research findings or in multidisciplinary teams)

- reflect on ways of becoming aware of your existing levels of personal knowledge about research and about substantive professional knowledge, ways of increasing that knowledge base and extending your personal skills and ways of relating to peer and group assessment
- explore ways of improving your ability to communicate your ideas and necessary information in oral presentations.

Introduction

Studying is often organized in social contexts (even distance learning courses tend to have points of contact between tutors and students and between students and their peers). Yet the possibilities of learning *through* the social aspects of the setting, as well as simply learning *within* it, are not always fully explored. If the interpretation of 'friends' originally intended by Emerson in the quote above is widened to include colleagues, peers and tutors then I think I can draw a parallel with the way in which many students from my own experience have treated those whom they encounter during the process of studying through and about research: they are there but they are seldom used. While it may seem somewhat calculating and manipulative to suggest that you conceive of your friends and colleagues as useful material for your own progression as a research student, I would argue that your learning can be enhanced by those around you. In this chapter I try to unravel the social dimension to learning for you as a returning student at research degree level.

Researching and communicating

Before I even begin to look at the detail of working and communicating with others it is worth stressing that, while research is an activity that *may* be conducted in private and with little intervention from others, most researchers would argue that sooner or later research work has to come out into the public domain, certainly this is so if it is to have any impact on the wider culture. Indeed, there is an underpinning ethic to doing research that suggests that it should be for the greater good, that in some way society at large should benefit (and that may be interpreted very broadly) from the findings of the researchers – else why do it at all? At the point of interface between you as a researcher, your findings and the world of others comes the need for communication.

Once again we are faced with a situation where research degree study differs from all the other forms of study that you may have been involved with in the past because, in this instance, it requires that you engage with those outside of your project who may or may not have an inherent interest in your work and who may or may not understand the methods you have employed and the implications of the findings your researching has produced. Communicating outcomes is a necessary aspect of research and because research degree study is done through researching then it also necessarily involves communication of methods and outcomes. This is not necessarily the case for all other forms of study where it is possible to conceive of someone learning in isolation, being examined in isolation and being awarded in isolation.

Above and beyond the necessary relationship between researching and communicating, many researchers would argue that their research practice is enhanced by the involvement of others. Again, there may be a disciplinary difference here but increasingly researchers across the disciplines are recognizing that lone research runs the risk of becoming sterile, while collaboration and critical appraisal by those outside of the project are generally seen as potentially enhancing. You only have to look at the number of renowned researchers and academic writers who work and publish in collaboration of one kind or another at some points in their careers to see that working and hence communicating with others is pervasive within the research and academic scenes, and for good reason.

In general, researchers need to bounce their ideas off others and need to receive feedback on what they have undertaken and written. That is why research journals, seminars and conferences are deemed so vital to the life blood of doing research. Research networking is not merely a social nicety, it is a way of engaging with the ideas and research practices of others. Research is perhaps best conceived as a process of dialogue between the researcher and other experts or researchers and the consumers of the research. For you as a research student there is then a need to talk with others to get feedback, to make connections between your work and that of others. In one sense this is a matter of integrating yourself and your ideas and methods into an academic community; and you should not underestimate the importance of this integration. This working with others begins with your supervisor(s) and works outward from there.

Working effectively in groups

Collaborative research

Working collaboratively on research projects may, in part, be a discipline-specific phenomenon. Certainly, in some of the sciences projects are so complex as to require that different aspects of an overall research aim need to be separated out into specific objectives to make the project manageable and these objectives in turn require research workings that are, in themselves, significant enough to warrant a research degree award (at one of the three levels already defined). Having noted some discipline specificity, I should add that collaborative research is becoming more and more common across the spectrum of intellectual disciples. Most university regulations will accommodate to this kind of collaborative process and again you should check out what your institution's regulations say in this respect. It is likely that for a research award to be made in this context, the examining panel would need to be provided with evidence: first, that a distinct contribution to the research has been made by the individual who is submitting for the award in question, and second, that this contribution is significant enough to meet the criteria for the award. The fact of any possible interdependence with the work of others in terms of the overall programme is not the prime issue, though it may be pursued legitimately in the context of the viva.

However, I think that there is an issue for you as a student in such a situation and it comes prior to the final assessment and relates to progress on 'your part' of the overall programme. I have known situations where a level of interdependence between components of a research project leads to one student becoming dependent on another's progress with his or her part of that project. For example, it may be that you find yourself waiting for the results of some aspect of the project that your collaborator is responsible for, and the 'waiting' is such that you cannot make progress yourself without access to the data that are being produced by your colleague. Here then you are in a difficult position where you are dependent on the progress of another for your own ultimate success.

What we need to do here is separate out success in the research project and success in gaining a research degree award. Though it may seem strange to say, these things are not necessarily the same – though clearly they are usually linked. In any collaborative research project you and your supervisor need to develop a sense of contingency awareness that your submission for an award should not be hindered by any breakdown in the collaboration to such an extent that a successful submission for the academic award in question becomes impossible. You need to retain an understanding that a research degree is, in part at least, a training in doing research. Where difficulties arise through collaboration you need to be able not only to show how you have learnt about researching from the experience but also to demonstrate 'contribution' at the level required by the award for which you are submitting. This may seem a hard task when the dependency was profound but it is what is needed and, though it may require some deep and divergent thinking, I would argue that is always possible to find a way of continuing to work so that you can demonstrate that you as a candidate have met the criteria for the award.

Roles and responsibilities of group members in research contexts

Whether or not it is overtly recognized, examples of group working are ubiquitous within research and research degree study. Often research projects demand teams, sometimes of individuals drawn from different disciplines and I think I can claim that, currently in the UK, research degree supervision always involves teams. In this latter respect it may be that you see and hear little from all the members of your supervisory team and you might think that this may or may not be to your benefit. It seems to me that not to make use of all members of your supervisory team is to lose out on some of the potential gains that such use may well bring about.

What is clear to me is that all members of your supervisory team do not have to play the same full part in your supervision – otherwise why would it be necessary to define one of your supervisors as 'main', 'principal' or as the 'director' of your studies? But in a team of two or three (or exceptionally more) each supervisor should have a defined role. It may be for example that a 'third' supervisor is used as someone who comes in with fresh eyes to look at the progress on a project at key points in the programme and to ask questions and act as a critical friend in this way. Alternatively it may be that one of your supervisory team brings a particular expertise to the project, statistical modelling for example, and is used primarily in this respect. It is hard for me in this text to define what might or might not be reasonable roles for individual team members to play within your specific supervisory team but it may suffice to note that they should have roles in your supervision and they should be available to you to fulfil them.

Accessing knowledge

Extant knowledge

In the literature about research degree study you will find much written about needing to push back the boundaries of knowledge and indeed I have made great play of this aspect of the study already in this book. But, of course, creating 'new' knowledge must begin with an understanding of the extant knowledge base. All research degree programmes need to be rooted in what is known, or has already been experienced, and such rooting requires that you become familiar with the field within which your proposed research project sits. Quite simply, you cannot expect to add to understanding within an intellectual field without first mapping out what is already known; you must know about existing boundaries if you are to know how and where you are going to push them back and so that you will be able to recognize that pushing back when you have done it.

A survey of what already exists is therefore essential in any research degree study and here I am talking about something more than a 'survey of the literature'; your surveying needs to be critical in analysing how and why things have been discovered to date in the way that they have. It is not enough to demarcate existing findings or to describe the state of the literature as it exists at present. You need to unravel the dynamic that inevitably exists between previous research activity and its attendant methodologies, and ideas, understandings and presumptions that have held sway in the past and those that now predominate. Knowledge and understanding are not static entities and therefore any survey that describes them as such will not be good enough to act as a basis for developing your own research ideas and activities. As a research student you must do more than map out what is already known; you have to analyse it in such a way as to enable you to demonstrate an intellectual platform for your own work and a reasonable projection for research activity.

Professional associations

If you are returning to study from a professional background the relevant professional organizations may be significant. They may act as repositories of knowledge and in some cases as gatekeepers for the development of knowledge in the sense that they may act to validate developments and may control to a greater or lesser extent the process of dissemination. For example, your professional organization may have sections which publish professional journals containing refereed articles (the process of refereeing is one of validation by peer review) and thus that organization acts as a conduit for the ideas and practical developments within that (professionally related) discipline. As a side issue I cannot resist noting that if Nietzsche was right when he wrote about knowledge 'working as a tool of power and increasing with every increase of power' then it may be assumed that a professional body that 'controls' knowledge (or indeed its dissemination) increases its own viability, power and independence within the wider social scene. But whatever the case it may be useful to think through the way in which you can use professional organizations, as appropriate, to help you to access knowledge and later to disseminate your own findings.

Information technology

There will almost inevitably have been advances in the speed and flexibility in communications since your last experience of study. An important dimension of your successful return then becomes a matter of finding out about the availability of new ways of accessing information. Indeed, as I write this section I am acutely aware that whatever forms of electronic communication I give as examples may well have been superseded by the time you read this text.

Clearly, the Internet often makes information accessible long before it is available in bookshops and libraries. Increasingly, for example, official reports and the results of findings from authorized investigations are posted on the Internet at the same time as they are released to the press and into bookshops. Getting information off the Internet and using it in your own writing can cause problems in terms of referencing your sources (material presented *only* in electronic form may be hard to claim as a source which is readily and permanently accessible within the public domain – which is the claim you can and do make when you reference or quote a source 'in the literature'). However, becoming knowledgeable requires that you make full use of all avenues for finding out the latest information and views – and the Internet is likely to be key in this respect. Indeed, it is not solely a matter of what material you can access from what is out there on the Internet, but also what you can share and what you can proactively find through the Internet. For example, you may want to consider creating your own web page if you are developing an interest in a particular area. Again, you would need to refer to a specialist text for information as to how to proceed but the difficulties might not be as daunting as you may think and the possibilities could be rewarding.

Suggestions for further reading

See Section 10 of Further Reading for texts that refer to accessing the Internet.

Fellow research students

I have already noted, when mentioning for example the possibilities inherent in such things as study syndicates and/or reading groups, how useful fellow students may be to you in your research degree studies. But it is worth focusing here on the fact that, again, research degree study differs from all other forms of university study in that it requires you to develop new skills that will enable you to become a creator of new understandings rather than merely a recipient of given knowledge. Such an active approach to knowledge requires that you engage with others who are similarly learning about research through doing it because you need them to act as reflectors for your own development as a researcher. At the end of research degree study (specifically at doctoral level though this applies to a lesser extent at other levels) you need to be able to understand the perspective of peers in relation to your research findings and the impact of those findings on them. The way to learn to do this is to engage with their perspectives and their reactions in terms of impact from the outset of your studies and throughout your programme of work. Working wholly in splendid isolation on a research project is not tenable where you have to learn about researching from engaging in that work – you need your (research degree) peers.

Accessing research techniques

One of the key aspects of becoming an effective research student, in the context of others with whom you are able to work and hence communicate, is the ways in which you can access a range of broad approaches to research and specific research methods from interactions with others. To become an effective researcher, or indeed a professional who makes effective use of research to improve his or her professional practice, you need to become familiar with different approaches to research and aware enough of their peculiarities, strengths and weaknesses to make use of them judiciously in the future. All too often those involved in doing research slip into a comfort zone where particular methods that prove effective for them in one situation are then transferred into future situations without due care and consideration for their continuing appropriateness. As in all other walks of life there is a danger, then, that people will prefer the familiar over the new and will base their predictions of usefulness on past experiences rather than on a critical analysis on an ongoing case by case basis. In the relatively short space of time available to you as a research student you need to gain access to as many examples of research in practice as you can. You need to exploit every opportunity to question not only what methods were chosen but also why they were chosen, how they were employed, how they have yielded findings and how the nature of the research design has affected what can be drawn from those findings.

It is difficult to give an example that will illustrate this point in a way that will cross disciplinary boundaries. Perhaps it is fair, however, to ask you to consider a research investigation within your own field within the frame of questions set out in the task – 'Analysing the research techniques of others'.

Task: analysing the research techniques of others

Take any research investigation within your field (published if necessary). Consider the following questions, not worrying for the moment about formal labelling of these things but rather focusing on what this means to you in your current state of understanding.

- What was the broad research approach taken (e.g. qualitative or quantitative, experimental or observation of natural occurrences)?
- What were the specific elements of the design within that broad approach (e.g. what specific statistical analyses were employed or what kinds of interview technique were used)?
- Can you identify any different outcomes that might have resulted if either the broad approach or the specific methods had been different (e.g. many more responses would have resulted if questionnaires had been used in preference to interviews)?

- Balance out advantages and disadvantages accruing from different approaches (e.g. using questionnaires would have given more responses overall but the researcher would have had less chance to check or verify answers or to pursue points of interest).

In answer to the third bit of the question, in the study I have just read I can see that if the researcher had asked the clients outright what they thought of the (drug rehabilitation) programme they were on then she would have got some very different answers than the ones she got from simply observing what they did during the programme. Of course, the answers might not have been any closer to the truth – for a start drug users are notorious for giving questioners what they think you want to hear – but they would have been different. I guess it's what you want to use the information you get for that makes a difference to whether, in this case, you ask or you observe.

(Psychiatric social worker, in the first year of a DProf programme)

It may also be the case in some disciplines that your time as a registered research student is an opportunity to engage at a practical level with specific research techniques in the laboratory or in the field. Sometimes there may be a tension for you, and indeed for your supervisor, in wishing to on the one hand explore a range of methods and techniques and on the other the need to make progress with the specific research project in hand, that is going to be the substantive part of your research degree submission. The tension here is best resolved on a case by case basis with advice from your supervisor. However, it is worth remembering that doing a research degree is a matter of engaging in being trained as a researcher; it is not solely a matter of doing a research project and 'cashing it in' for an award (though it may feel like this at times). Learning to be a researcher should not become a narrow matter; your learning of research in such a way as to enable you to become an effective independent researcher in the future, as described above, is paramount.

Suggestions for further reading
See Section 2 of Further Reading for works that make reference to the learning of specific research skills and methods.

Oral presentations

Oral presentations in the professional context

One of the more clearly defined and significant aspects of working and communicating with others is the giving of oral presentations. Before I discuss some of the detail of giving such presentations I want to make the link between what you may do in your work outside of academia and what formal research degree study may demand of you. If you are involved in a professional setting, your work may involve some kind of interface with colleagues where you are required to convey your views, findings or conclusions and increasingly the interface may extend to other professional and non-professional areas. You may therefore already have experience of public speaking in one form or another and it may be a matter of drawing on that experience and adapting what you have learnt for the (new) academic purpose of making oral presentations about your research degree studies.

You may have experienced different kinds of pressure when speaking to those from within your own intellectual discipline and/or professional background when compared with speaking to a lay audience. This is not to suggest that either one is inherently more difficult than the other but that accepted knowledge of technical language and level of ability and understanding as well as perspective on, and likely attitude towards, issues will necessarily affect the way in which you approach the task of presenting ideas. What you need to do here is to reflect upon why there should be a difference between what is required of you by different audiences and what you have learnt about your own difficulties and potentials in talking to groups of people. Without wishing to overcategorize, it may be possible to conceive of audiences as being 'lay', professional or research oriented. Then, of course, there are those in audiences who will be both professional and aware of, and interested in, relevant research – even though they do not themselves engage actively in researching. My only purpose in differentiating here is to underline the obvious point that whenever one speaks to an audience the first thing you need to do is to recognize their background, likely existing understanding and, most importantly, their expectations of you as a speaker – what have they come to listen to. Considering effectively the needs of the audience is the first step to a successful presentation. This is not to say, of course, that giving an audience something different from their expectation is a necessarily a negative thing, but it needs to be handled with care.

Structuring of oral presentations about your research

In any oral presentation about your research you need to clarify for yourself what the main points are that you wish to convey, how you will introduce your topic and how you will draw it to a conclusion. Then you need to put yourself in the position of the listeners and decide how what is already clear to you can become clear to them. It may be that you need to set out the skeleton of the talk for them at the outset, giving them an organization of the whole talk in advance and then proceeding to fill in the detail. You might do this verbally, or more likely you will use some kind of visual representation (e.g. an outline in bullet points shown on an overhead projector or a flow diagram showing how the ideas and investigations will come together as you talk). If this approach is to be used then you can develop it into an ongoing structuring in which you remind your listeners of where you have got to in the overall plan, reverting if appropriate to the original visual representation. Also, you have the option of using the same original visualization as the summary (e.g. *'These, then, are the key aspects of the research projects and its results that I have covered'*).

It is often the case within the research world that your presentation will be one of several, with each having an allotted slot and each following hard on the heels of the previous. In this kind of staccato world, where complex ideas are put across in rapid succession, setting out clearly what you are to say, saying it as coherently as possible and then summarizing succinctly are all important if the audience is to be able to grasp your ideas quickly and effectively (i.e. in the brief amount of time available to them).

Using notes during an oral presentation

One of the first issues that needs resolving is the degree of formality of the talk (e.g. will there be an ongoing dialogue with the audience or not?) and the possibility and appropriateness of using notes (and the extent of note use). A general rule of thumb that I apply in my own work is that the more I rely on the reading of notes then the less natural my presentation will seem and the less engaging it is likely to be for the audience. Of course, there are occasions where, literally, 'reading a paper' is the appropriate format. The judgement must be yours but it is an important one which has significant implications for the way in which your presentation is likely to be received. Most researchers would probably agree that it is more difficult to engage with the ideas a speaker is trying to get across when he or she is reading from a script rather than speaking naturally. Equally, however, listening to someone who is talking about his or her research in an unfocused and unstructured way can be frustrating. A useful compromise that many colleagues use is to have a written talk, which is then reduced to a series of points. These points can be written on cards and used as prompts. This approach enables you to adhere to some kind of academic rigour when discussing your research and at the same time retain the naturalness that aids accessibility for your audience. A variation on this theme is to 'talk to' a PowerPoint® presentation and I return to this possibility in a separate section below.

Practising oral presentations

A practice enables you to work out what you are to say at each stage of the talk (in relation to each acetate or slide if you are using such), make sure that the sequencing of ideas or major points is appropriate, and confirm that your estimations of timing are reasonably accurate. On this last point of timing I should point out that rehearsing a presentation silently 'in your head' is unlikely to give you an accurate indication of timing – you will tend to take longer when you come to actually speak the words. My own early experiences of giving talks about my research were very much a matter of learning just how difficult it is to judge the time it will take to deliver a given amount of material. I am not sure even now that there are any shortcuts to knowing how long a talk will take to deliver. The real answer to the problem perhaps is to be flexible in what you expect to cover. For example, sometimes I include sections in my prepared material that can be cut, without losing the sense of the whole, if I judge as I talk that time is running short. In other talks I have different end points and I stop at a convenient one when my allotted time runs out. Of course, my audience does not need to know that sections have been cut or that there are different endings (unless of course they have them on a PowerPoint handout); it is hoped that what they see and hear is an apparently complete performance which comes to an end naturally at a predetermined time. (I used, on occasions, to comment on the fact that I was having to miss parts out because of pressure of time and would set aside acetates with a flourish – until this once provoked a member of the audience to point out to me in the coffee break, 'You know, we are all desperate to know what was on the acetates you didn't use'.)

Observing other speakers

In the same way that it is important to look at other people's writing that you value and try to learn how they get across ideas, structure the reporting of their research, phrase their sentences etc., so it can be very profitable for you to pay attention to how someone you perceive to be a good speaker works at his or her task. A successful oral research presentation does not happen by magic; although it may seem effortless it will inevitably be the result of experience, learned skills and careful thought and preparation. You need to become not only an observer of what is being said by the good speaker but also a student of *how* it is being said – asking yourself how it is that the speaker is so convincing and understandable, how he or she employs strategies to clarify ideas, gain and hold the attention of the audience and so on. Watching a consummate performer is an opportunity for you to learn about the art of performance as well as about the particular content concerned. It is sometimes tempting to admire a good speaker as a 'natural' and to assume that he or she has gifts of oratory that you could never match. Yet all speakers learn the craft of public speaking; even the best will have got to the stage you are admiring through effort and learning (though admittedly some will have learnt more readily than others) and talking about research is no different from any other form of oratory.

The final point I need to make here is that when you observe others speaking, particularly perhaps those who seem effortlessly in command, all may not always be as it seems. For example, speakers who appear to be talking in an unplanned, spontaneous way may well have rehearsed their spontaneity quite carefully; as Mark Twain once acknowledged, 'It usually takes me more than three weeks to prepare a good impromptu speech.'

Task: learning from a good example
- Recall an example of a presenter who impressed you as a good speaker or better still one instance of a talk that you thought to be good.
- Note down features of the speaker or the talk which you think contributed to its quality.
- Can you adapt any of these features for your own use in your own oral presentations?

The features of the good talk were: confidence, eye contact, presence, elaborating (off the cuff) from single points. I think the researcher had prepared thoroughly – I need to adapt her 'knowing the subject confidently and not giving it in too much detail'. Above all I need to practise.
(Information scientist registered for an MSc by research)

I think it was pace really. She kept my attention by somehow varying the speed at which she talked. It was something to do with the way she led up to a point then summarized it for me then started again and slowly built up to the next one. That and the fact that she was funny – without seeming to tell jokes she made me laugh. I think it was the way she said what she said rather than what she said in itself.
(Environmental scientist registered for a PhD)

Recognizing the constraints on your oral presentation

A significant aspect of planning and practice is recognition of the limitations of the research talk you are to give. In particular you will be limited by time and by the capabilities of your audience; this is not to denigrate your likely audience but to stress that no audience can cope with too many ideas or facts presented in too short a time (and I have already noted that the research world is permeated by hectic sequences of short presentations). These two limitations combine to create perhaps the most significant aspect of your advance organization and rehearsal: the need to cover a limited number of key ideas or components of information in the specified time without undue haste. My own rules of thumb are that in a 20 minute talk I reckon to cover only two or three main ideas or themes (subdivided of course) and that ideally no talk should last for more than 50 minutes (without some kind of natural 'break'). Certainly, I have found that the ability of an audience to listen and actively attend to detail will diminish as time and more presented ideas increase. It will help to recognize this and, where a long talk is required, respond as follows:

- Alert the audience to the structure of the talk before you begin.
- Break up your 'text' into sections that enable the audience to accommodate new ideas systematically.
- Present ideas in a thematic way with reminders of what you have just covered and signposts to indicate where you are leading your listeners.
- Break up your talk with tasks for the audience to do or opportunities for them to discuss points with others or ask you questions of clarification before you go on to the next section or point.
- Return full circle to the main issues at the end of the presentation by way of summary.

Using overhead transparencies and slides or PowerPoint®

Research presentations are very often accompanied by overhead transparencies (sometimes referred to as acetates) or slides or PowerPoint (electronic system of 'slides' run from a laptop or similar) because they offer the speaker visual props for his or her spoken words. Most of what I say in this section applies to all the formats mentioned above; however, PowerPoint does present some particular issues and therefore I will deal with it in a separate paragraph below.

All the formats for visual representations give the audience something to focus on as well as the spoken word. My own presentations tend to revolve around my PowerPoint 'slides' and I devote the majority of preparation time to writing and refining them. I use them as an aide-mémoire in much the same way as other colleagues use cards as mentioned earlier. It seems to me then that it is hard to overstate the importance of a good set of visuals as the basis for a successful talk. You need to develop your use of them to suit your own style of delivering an oral presentation but some general guidance might be offered as follows:

- Slides should be kept simple with as few words used as possible.
- Always use a big typeface, in bold, and make sure that your words are readable from the back of the room.
- Use diagrammatic information where it can usefully summarize and therefore replace text.
- Use bullet points or their equivalent.
- An overview of the whole talk at the outset on one slide is helpful in setting the scene and enabling the listeners to organize their attention in advance of your spoken words.

- Avoid standing in front of the screen as you speak.
- Avoid speaking 'to' the screen with your back to the audience.

PowerPoint (or pretty much any other form of computer-generated 'slide show') is worth special note, perhaps, in the range of visual prompts mentioned inasmuch as it allows: the importing of a seemingly unending list of graphic stimuli available electronically, the use of colours, movements and sounds, and the employment of all kinds of figurative representations, tabular representations and so on. In my own view its apparent strengths also carry its hidden dangers. It is possible to do the following:

- Add in pretty much any visual or auditory representation that you want.
- Create large numbers of slides without much mechanical effort.
- 'Animate' your slides (e.g. so that words fly onto the screen from various directions in a whole host of different ways and diffuse in, perhaps, scatter patterns when you have finished with them).
- Build in flexibility in how you present your talk (e.g. you can go forwards and backwards and skip slides at will).

But in each of these apparent strengths there lies a danger:

- Your audience may begin to feel a sense of stimulation overload from too many visual representations that begin to get in the way of the audience's understanding.
- You may end up trying to present far too much information simply because it is so easy to include it (the current expression that audiences often use is 'death by PowerPoint').
- Animation can seem attractive at first but can become distracting for an audience that becomes engrossed in where words are next about to fly in from rather than what they mean.
- Skipping forwards and backwards can be disorientating for an audience that finds itself watching words that it has already seen flash before its eyes in reverse order.

Reflecting on a research presentation

It is important that you make the most use of every opportunity to give a research paper and this means that you need to reflect carefully, following your presentations – otherwise you may not learn as much as is possible from the experience. In the task 'Reflecting on a research presentation following its delivery' I have set out the kinds of questions that might help structure your reflection.

Task: reflecting on a research presentation following its delivery

When you have finished speaking you need to reflect on your performance and the efficacy of your supporting materials. For example, you might ask yourself (or your supervisor or a peer if possible) the followings kinds of question:

- Did the sections of my talk enable the audience to understand quickly enough, and subsequently follow easily enough, the structure of my presentation?
- Did the visual parts of my talk (e.g. PowerPoint) help the audience to understand my points?
- Did I try to get in too much or too little information?
- Was my presentation rushed in any way and if so why (note that this may or may not relate to the previous question about amount of material covered)?
- Did what I presented match audience expectations of the talk?
- Could the audience hear me and see me clearly enough?
- Did I allow them chance to ask questions to clarify any misunderstandings?

To say that my presentation was rushed would be a massive understatement. I totally misjudged how long it would take to get through each slide. I was worried that I would not have enough to say and that I would dry up with time left at the end. But I simply had too many. In the event, somebody in the front row asked if he could ask a question when I was about two slides in and I said 'Yes' because I felt it would look cowardly if I said no. He proceeded to make a speech that seemed to go on for ever with a question stuck in somewhere at the end – I got flustered and a bit sidetracked in trying to answer him and I think that was where a lot of the time went. In any case, when I looked at the clock a few minutes later I was horrified to see that my time was almost up. I hurried through as many of the remaining slides as I could.

(Second year PhD student doing research into financial management)

After all of this you need to remember the basic maxims of all public speaking: stand up, tell your audience what you are about to tell them, then tell them what you come to say as economically as you can, then tell your audience what you have just told them and sit down. Or as Franklin D. Roosevelt would have it, 'Be sincere; be brief; be seated.' Indeed, brevity is often hard to attain in a research paper but invaluable if you can manage it.

Suggestions for further reading

See Section 4 of Further Reading for publications that refer to giving oral research presentations.

Relationships with tutors or supervisors (both academic and work based)

Particularity of the student–tutor relationship in the professional context

If you are returning to study while maintaining your professional work, I think it is helpful to consider the kinds of relationships that are likely to exist between you as a professional and your academic tutors or supervisors. For example, there may be serious and complex ethical issues which need to be taken into account when you embark on any kind of research investigation in your professional workplace. These may relate to matters of confidentiality relating to clients or to issues of possible 'abuse of power' if your researching requires that you analyse and discuss in seminars, or in written reports and ultimately in your final submission, working relationships and practices that involve those working for you in a supporting role. Again, a hallmark of many professions is that care and concern for the clients is paramount; if there is any possibility that your engaging in research study may be to the detriment of your clients (perhaps because you are focusing on your own need to reflect on professional practice in order to gain an academic award rather than their needs as clients) then clearly you may be in conflict with your own professional standards and etiquette. Usually, of course, there is no conflict and successful research study and 'professional work of benefit to the client group' are synonymous.

Codes of Practice and Notes of Guidance

In terms of trying to ensure that you derive the most benefit out of the course of research study on which you embark it is worth mentioning the expectations you are entitled to hold of the institution in which you study and research and similarly the expectations it will hold, legitimately, of you. Commonly, practices will be defined within a university that are accepted as minimum requirements or guidelines will be given as to the way in which supervisors and research students should operate and co-operate. Codes of Practice for Research Students and Notes of Guidance should give you some idea of what you can expect in terms of, for example, time allocated for supervision meetings, the availability of resources and the nature and extent of feedback. While such documents may seem of low priority in the early stages of registration and acclimatization to research degree study, it may help you get the most out of the institution if you read through them before you become embroiled in the various aspects of research study. You need to know what is expected of you so that (assuming it is reasonable) you can do your best to deliver and to know what you can expect of the institution so that you can make the best use of what is available. Again, I believe this to be true for all students but for those returning to study for a research degree the need is paramount for the reasons I have already given in this book – namely that research degree study requires of you a particular and sharply defined role in driving forward your own programme of research degree study. Quite simply, if you are to be active successfully in this respect you need to be aware of the rules under which you are operating.

Suggestions for further reading

It might help you to better understand the complexities of relationships with your supervisors if you read some of the publications listed in Section 5 of Further Reading. Some of the texts cited there are written for supervisors but this of course may give you some insight into how they approach the supervisory situation.

Summary

- You have considered how you might approach issues of working effectively in the kinds of group situations that are operative in your professional setting and the kinds of group learning situations that you are likely to encounter in your return to research degree study.
- You have thought of ways of increasing your awareness of your own knowledge and skills in relation to research and the possibilities for increasing it.
- You have considered how you might improve your communication during oral research presentations.
- You have thought about how you can make the most of working relationships with other research students and academic staff.

Conclusion

How similar are you to Ralph Emerson in your treatment of friends and colleagues: do you like to know that they are there but seldom if ever make the most of them? My first theme in this chapter has been that you need to recognize the way in which your work outside of academia brings you into contact with groups and individuals both professional and non-professional and what you need to do to make yourself a more effective social operator in these contexts. I have suggested that the first step to improvement may be in recognition of realities and possibilities: what goes on in these respects in your (professional) life and what can you do about it (assuming something needs to be done). My second theme has been that working with others is likely to be an integral part of your return to research degree study and that, given this to be the case, it may be helpful to interpret group learning situations in academia as useful opportunities to enhance your own performance as a learner as well as to learn specific content about research methods effectively.

6

Planning to do your research

Research is the process of going up alleys to see if they are blind.
Marston Bates (1906–1974)

Overview

Embarking on a research degree programme will involve you in levels and kinds of planning with which you may not be familiar. In this chapter, therefore, you will be asked to:

- consider what is distinctive about planning a research degree
- analyse your part in the planning process
- think about what needs to be done by way of preparing for the continuity of your research throughout the course of your research programme
- come to terms with the various pitfalls and possible delays that may occur in the planning stage.

Introduction

I am not sure that I entirely endorse the sentiments that underlie the quotation from Bates above, or rather I would not wish you to interpret it to mean
that research is simply a matter of wandering up one alley after another in the
hope that one of them will lead you somewhere that you might want to go.
Of course, Bates does not refer to 'wandering' in any sense and one can perhaps legitimately assume that he had something altogether more systematic
in mind. In my view there has to be some purpose in going up each of the
kinds of research alleys that Bates has in mind, and whether or not you decide
to investigate something, or something in a particular way, should be a decision that is resolved by careful planning. Effective research requires first and
foremost that you work out in advance, inasmuch as you can, what will be
required of you, your resources and (where applicable) your clients, subjects
or participants. Venturing up metaphorical alleys is part of the reality of the
research world and I think Bates was right to draw attention, with his analogy
of alleyways, to the notion that research involves the investigation of possibilities, that is, of possible solutions to problems and possible interpretations
of phenomena. But what is also clear to me is that there is a need to prepare
carefully for such exploration. As a student learning about how to research,
you need to learn the place of preparation in the kind of exploration to which
Bates draws our attention.

The distinctiveness of planning within a research degree

When studying for a research degree you are not following an academic path
set down by others who are assumed to know better than you what you need
to study and indeed how you are to study. When you register for such a degree
there is no syllabus that you can follow. What you need to study is dependent
on the demands of your research programme in order that you complete the
research effectively. Yet of course this is not so straightforward in practice
because you may need to study some things in order to define the limits of
your research. When you submit your research degree work for assessment you
have to justify why you did *not* look at a particular aspect of the problem or
why you looked at it in one way and not in another. This requires therefore
that you become conversant with methodologies and aspects of the substantive area that may be outside of the direct concerns of your final submission to
the extent that you know (and are able to defend) why they were not included
in your eventual programme of research. All of this contrasts sharply with
taught course work where the delineating of the boundaries of what must be

known and how it must be learnt are, largely at least, defined prior to the learner arriving on the scene.

Preparatory and preliminary work

When I came to write this section and divide it into subsections my tidy mind conceived of my task as setting out for you some kind of linear process through which you might go in order to prepare yourself for the research work ahead. But as I worked through the subsections I became increasingly aware that these things are not sequential. I can separate them out here for the purpose of presenting them to you tidily but in reality what you do first and second and so on will depend on various factors that I cannot account for here and in any case preparation is a whole event: you might choose a topic and then read about it or a topic might arise from your reading, you might spend some time narrowing down the topic to be investigated and hence the kinds of investigation that will be involved or you might realize that the kinds of investigation that are possible (given limits on time, resources or access to subjects) necessarily narrows down the topic for you. In short, the sections below are not necessarily to be encountered sequentially – they are often inter-changeable, always interrelated and sometimes interdependent. The next two sections perhaps exemplify this most clearly.

Choosing a topic

Here is a good example of what I tried to explain above. In placing 'choosing a topic' before 'preparatory reading' I am not suggesting that you choose a topic and then read about it. Of course this may happen for various reasons but equally it may not. The choice of topic might be refined in the process of reading or indeed of reading, investigating and then further reading. In short, the process of narrowing down a topic for investigation is an organic one and should involve some iterations of ideas, comment, testing or reading, ideally between you and your supervisor. There is no rule of thumb about how long this process should take – it varies between disciplines and according to the topic itself. Indeed, sometimes the refining of a question or a methodology may be a substantial part of the final submission (and hence an integral part of the 'contribution to knowledge').

There are however some things that are worth considering in any (research degree) topic choice:

- Is it achievable by you, in the time available, and with the resources available?
- Is it likely to lead to a contribution to knowledge (if operating at doctoral

level) – or a 'contribution' at whatever level of award you are studying. This would involve, at doctoral level at least, the question 'Has it been done before?', i.e. is it original?

- Is it reasonable to expect that any findings will be significant enough for the level of award (e.g. is the impact on professional practice likely to be substantial enough to lead practitioners to engage in their work with new ideas or (intellectual) tools; another way of looking at this is to ask 'might the findings be of the kind that are publishable in an appropriate location' (this would vary between level of award and kind of award, e.g. between a PhD and a professional doctorate)?
- Is it ethical?

It is worth expanding on these bullet points below.

Achievable by you?

Research projects involve the researcher in the use of various personal skills, some of which are non-technical and may seem trivial but nevertheless may be significant to the success of the project and most of which are predictable at the outset. For example, if your project requires that you interview vulnerable children then you need to have the sensitivity, and in some instances a professional training, to be able to carry out those interviews successfully – to be comfortable in working in what may be emotionally challenging circumstances. Similarly, if your investigations require fieldwork in physically challenging environments then you have to be able to cope with that challenge. At a different level, if your investigations are likely to require complex statistical analysis then you need to feel willing and able to learn the techniques necessary and subsequently operate, understand and defend the analyses involved.

In my experience, not all research projects are suitable for all research degree candidates, and vice versa, and there is a sense in which it is the joint responsibility of you and your supervisor to 'match-up' project with candidate in such a way that takes account of compatibility issues and thus ensures that the most likely outcome is a successful one. Your part of the responsibility hangs largely on honesty – both with yourself and with your supervisor – about your strengths and weaknesses as well as about your capabilities for learning.

Contribution to knowledge?

In the haste to make sure that you can get started on some investigation that is likely to yield reasonable results it is important that you and your supervisor keep sight of the main aim of all this – that you will have something to submit for the award for which you are registered (or intend to register in those institutions where development of the project precedes formal registration). I have already run through the levels of research degree award and so do not need here to revisit them; it is perhaps helpful however if I take the doctoral level criterion 'contribution to knowledge' (or local variations as appropriate). This notion of contribution is vital to research degree study yet it is also something that is hard to define, particularly in advance of a project actually being undertaken. It is also hard, on occasions, to identify or recognize even when the work is completed and, where there are disputes between examiners, it is often on the crucial matter of whether or not such a contribution has been made.

It may seem daunting then, for you as a research student starting out on your programme of studies, to have to think about and justify proposed work in terms of its likely contribution. Yet, of course, a university would be remiss in its duty to you if it allowed you to embark on a course of research work that is unlikely to produce the required 'contribution'. So, what you and your supervisor are doing at this stage is trying to decide what the likely outcomes are, of a proposed research programme, in terms of contribution. This therefore is a matter of setting out a reasonable trajectory for the work rather than defining its outcomes in detail (clearly if you could do that it would not be real research); it is a matter of proposing something that is in the right direction and has enough safeguards within it to give it the kind of internal integrity that justifies the claim that it carries within it the clear potential to deliver in terms of contribution.

One simple rule of thumb that may help you here is that, for a contribution to be made, your audience has to be able to learn something from reading your work and listening to your defence that they did not know before. 'Audience' in this sense would be, at PhD level, a group of experts in the field – the notion of expert includes the understanding that they would know what is already known and hence if they learn something that is new from your work then you have contributed to what is known. If your work is towards a professional doctoral award then your audience might well be expert professionals who will be judging whether or not your work has contributed to their understanding of some aspect of professional work and hence has contributed to the practice of that profession, i.e. your work will need to speak to and inform professional practitioners. At MPhil and masters levels the notion of contribution is likely to be lessened and here you need to read the specific regulations of your university to fully appreciate your target in this respect.

Significance of contribution?

Most university regulations pertaining to research degrees will contain some mention of the significance of the contribution to knowledge that is being made and again, as mentioned in earlier chapters, where it is mentioned this will most probably be a variable across the levels of research degree award (for example, though it is very hard to define, an MPhil is likely to require a lower level of significance than a PhD). As doctoral level is, perhaps, the one by which the other levels are measured I will use it as my example. Clearly significance, in the context of a doctoral award at least, is not a concept that is readily definable. Perhaps the simplest way of understanding it is to note that the experts who will examine your work may be informed by all sort of things in their working day and reading your work may be informative to them in a way that falls within their normal professional or academic practice (that is, the contributing is of a non-significant kind). For the 'informing' to become significant enough for a research degree to be awarded upon the basis of it, then it would need to shift the experts' views on the topic in hand to the extent that they are enabled to see it, and go on to investigate it for themselves, in a new light. In this way, examiners should leave the examination room with a feeling that the research they have interrogated has given them new insights which will in turn inform their own future research. This may seem a tall order for you as a student setting out on a research degree but it is the essence of the beast.

Is the research ethical?

There is not room in this book to deal with all the aspects of doing research ethically that might apply to all research projects in all disciplines. There are specialist texts for the purpose (see 'Further reading' below). However, it is important to stress the basic principles and to note that ethical consideration should permeate every aspect of the design, implementation and reporting of your research. You would be unwise to assume that 'ethics' do not apply to you on the grounds that your research does not involve doing anything invasive to people (e.g. testing new drug treatments on volunteers). The ethics of what you are proposing need consideration from the outset whether you are 'using' people or not. It might help here if I list some of the aspects of doing research for an academic award that do require ethical consideration, if only to indicate by way of examples the range of issues involved.

- All studies involving what are commonly termed 'human subjects' will, almost undoubtedly, require formal permission to proceed from a university 'ethics committee' or similar. In this context you would be wise to interpret 'human subjects' as including all human participants. That means that the interpretation includes: people who answer questionnaires, people in the street whose opinions are canvassed, people who are studied without their knowledge, volunteers, and people (e.g. clients) on whom you may test out ideas (e.g. a new professional procedure for dealing with client demand).
- In many professional contexts, perhaps most notable in hospital or care settings, there may well be national ethical guidelines (e.g. ethical codes from organizations such as the British Psychological Society) that must be followed in any kind of research and 'local' committees to which application for approval to proceed must be made.
- All studies involving animals (laboratory type work will be covered by Home Office regulations).
- All studies where analysis of any kind of personal data is involved.
- The reporting of findings where there may be an impact on participants

(due concern must be shown for the effects (intended and unintended) of reported findings on all concerned).
- The possible effects on professional colleagues of those aspects of your professional work that form part of your research degree studies.

You would be unwise to assume that your research is 'harmless' simply because it is designed only to help others and not in any way to interfere with them. Good intentions do not obviate the need to consider the implications of your research for others. I am not saying, of course, that any research projects falling within any of the areas outlined above will be unethical but rather that you need to think actively through the ethical implications of what you do and, where appropriate, apply for formal approval at the planning stage of your research programme.

Apart from the inherent importance of making sure that what you research and the way that you go about it are within the boundaries of what is ethically acceptable, there are practical considerations. I have seen a number of students get into difficulties, specifically over the timing of their work, because they have quite simply not applied for ethical approval and have been stopped from undertaking work or have not applied early enough and have, in their own terms, 'wasted' valuable time. You need to build in attention to the ethical dimension from the beginning through to the end of your programme of study. Without wishing to sound like a harbinger of doom, many institutions will have regulations in force that enable them to block the award of a research degree or even overturn the outcome of an examination where it is (later) proven that the research undertaken transgressed its own guidelines for the ethical behaviour of researchers. In such cases ignorance of the rules is no defence.

You have to ensure that your research project is designed so that no harm (intentional or unintentional) is likely to come to anyone as a result of what you do and how you report what you do. My own view is that there are some projects that are simply not viable because the intended aims cannot be realized without a real risk to someone at some point in the process (again from the inception of investigations up to, and including, the reporting of findings). This view is complementary to my belief that all research that forms part of a research degree submission must be made publicly available and that there can be no exceptions (though there might, exceptionally, be a time limited embargo where commercial sensitivities are involved). There is an underpinning ethic to doing research that implies that findings must be shared with others (in the first instance for the purposes of public verification and in the second as a matter of the 'greater good'). The importance of this publicly available dimension here is that, in my view, you cannot sidestep issues of potential harm to participants by asserting that your reported findings need to be kept confidential by your university; such confidentiality flies in the face of what research, and more particularly doing a research degree, is all about.

Suggestions for further reading
See Oliver (2003), as referenced in Section 2 of Further Reading, for discussion on the ethics of doing research.

Task: defining a topic for investigation
As you begin to refine a notion of what your research project will involve, try to answer these questions.

- Are the goals you are setting out achievable
  - by you
  - in the time available
  - with the resources available
  - with likely access to a sufficient sample or data set?
- Is your project likely to lead to a contribution to knowledge (if operating at doctoral level) or a 'contribution' at whatever level of award you are studying? This would involve, at doctoral level at least, the question 'Has it been done before?', i.e. is it original?
- Is it reasonable to expect that any findings will be significant enough for the level of award (see examples in the text)?
- Is your project ethical?

I really came unstuck with my project when I couldn't get the time I had been promised on the radio telescope. There were obviously some politics going on in the department and I became a victim – my supervisor shouldn't have assumed we'd get the time but then I guess I was naive to expect it. Anyway the problem completely scuppered the work in my second year. I'm not sure even now how I got away with it. I did so little simply because I couldn't get access to the equipment. Getting the resources to do what we had all agreed I would do was my one big problem.

(Astronomy student having just been given 'substantial amendments' to a PhD submission)

I did a lot of work, everyone said that, my lab notes were full and I read a lot. I did a lot of teaching of undergraduates as well and I was good at that. But towards the end when I had to give a paper, the head of department said that it was all very interesting and he admired my enthusiasm but then asked me what my actual contribution was and I was completely flummoxed. It was hard to pin it down. When I came to write the thesis I found it even harder. My supervisor helped me shape it up so that I said something that I guess was new but I was never sure it was that important.

In the event the viva was a nightmare because that was the question they started with. Strangely, it was then that they, between them, came up with ideas about how I could do some more fairly simple studies which kind of turned my work into something that was worthwhile. It all seemed so obvious then – and I had to go away and do it. That's what I'm doing now – what I guess I should have done a couple of years ago. I am a hard worker and I'm sure it'll pay off. I know I can do it, I just wish I'd done it earlier – asked the hard question 'What's my contribution to the subject?' I'm sure I could have done it earlier.

(PhD student working on a resubmission in metallurgy)

Preparatory reading

In the light of the above, one of the key issues for you as a returning student, and indeed for your research degree supervisor, in the early stages of your registration is how to delineate the task ahead, what to read by way of preparation and when to stop such preparatory reading and engage actively in investigating a research topic. I have drawn a distinction here between preparatory reading and researching that may be misleading in some disciplines where the boundaries are blurred in this respect. Indeed, I would always argue that reading should never stop through the process of research degree study; even at the stage of preparing for the final oral examination you need to continue your reading to ensure that you are as up-to-date with the current literature as is possible. But the point of the distinction I have tried to make above is about *preparatory* reading – I am suggesting that you need to read around the subject enough to establish general familiarity (usually taken to be a necessary characteristic of a successful research degree candidate) and enough to understand the specific topic sufficiently well so as to enable you to design a reasonable investigative study that holds the potential to yield worthwhile findings.

There are two dangers here for you as a student. The first is that you may spend too long in reading around the subject to the extent that your start on carrying out investigations is unduly delayed (supervisors may see this as prevarication or as avoidance of the real task in hand). The second is that you are too hasty to 'get on with the research' and end up working on a project that is ill founded at best and misguided at worst.

Two contrasting student views on the initial stages of developing research degree ideas give examples of both dangers.

Looking back on it now I guess I spent far too long reading up about all these different aspects of my topic (children's learning about maths from the Internet) and putting off actually doing something. I kept finding more and more interesting things to read up about. I called it my research but after six months I realized that I had nothing to show for it except a card file with lots of cross-references and lots of yellow stickers with ideas scribbled on – I had not actually done anything – at least nothing I could point to as a 'product'. I think I was a bit scared of the idea of investigating something and it seemed safer to keep on reading and developing ideas – but in that first awful period I never got to testing them out. At the time I blamed my supervisor for not giving me some simple little investigations to get me started but looking back on it now I am not so sure.

(PhD student having successfully completed her award, looking back to when she started)

I knew what I wanted to do before I registered so I didn't feel the need to read much or even think about it much. I had some experiments in mind and my supervisor seemed impressed and happy for me to get on – so I did. It was only later when I started to write the literature review that I realized that other people had had similar thoughts and that some of my ideas had in fact already been tested out – or at least more or less – enough to make me rethink what I had already done. I wasted a lot of that first year that way.

(EngD student at the start of his second year of study, writing in his research log)

It may seem to you that the two dangers outlined above mean that you are damned if you do (spend too much time on a preparatory reading phase) and damned if you don't (spend not enough time on the preparatory reading phase). Of course, this is where supervisory guidance should be useful to you. Supervisors should be experienced enough to give appropriate advice on how to spend the early parts of your programme of research degree study. Clearly, there will be disciplinary differences in how that time is spent; nevertheless it may be possible to define the principles upon which decisions can be made regarding how to spend valuable time. In preparing the ground for the research work you are to undertake you need to search the literature:

- Establish what is known about the broad area of concern and how it relates to the specific topic chosen.
- Establish how your chosen topic (or the topic that is emerging from your reading) fits within the broad area of concern.
- Begin to make a judgement about how outcomes from your study might impact on the existing field and the existing understandings about your chosen topic.

Preparatory investigation

Preparatory investigation as part of a successful balance

There is often a balance to be struck, during the early stages of a research degree programme, between continuing to plan in detail a series of major studies that will form the substantial part of a submission, and beginning to carry out investigations, albeit of a preliminary and exploratory kind. Again, the sense of balance will vary according to the level of research degree award that you are undertaking (e.g. some masters by research programmes may consist of a number of exploratory studies in which the aim is for you to experience a range of kinds of methodology) as well as the discipline within which you are working. In a similar way to that noted in the above section on 'Preparatory reading', there are contrasting dangers here for you as a student. Sometimes, continuing to plan can become a matter of prevarication and/or a matter of frustration for you as a student who has signed up, and wants, to engage in (practical) research investigations. On the other hand, plunging too quickly into studies that are ill founded can lead to frustrating dead ends and unusable results. You need to seek guidance from your supervisory team on this matter, but I would say that I have known a number of occasions where my own students have benefited from engaging in quick exploratory studies where they have been able to learn about the difficulties of, for example, researching with particular client groups and in specific workplace contexts. Such learning has helped them become more realistic about the kinds of major studies that will be possible and fruitful. Research degrees are about learning to do research and, in one sense at least, the best way to learn is to do research – on however small and exploratory a level. I recall my own supervisor telling me, '*It'll be good for you to get your hands dirty.*' He was speaking metaphorically of course but he was right; learning by doing is a powerful device even at research degree level.

Pragmatic concerns at the preparatory investigation stage

There are, of course, a host of reasons why you may need and/or want to engage in some preparatory investigations before embarking on major research projects. In one sense you may need to investigate aspects of your overall topic in order to do the things that are suggested as necessary in the section above on 'Choosing a topic'. For example, you may need to do the following:

- Clear the ground by discounting some variables or by selecting out the kind of sample or population that you need to investigate in more detail later.
- Clarify the meaning of certain terms that are apposite within your overall topic.
- Scope out what archival material is available by an initial survey before beginning to analyse.
- Test out the responsiveness of certain methods or resources or equipment in the circumstances in which you intend to use them more fully.
- Test out your own abilities to deliver research outcomes of the kind that you intend to work towards more extensively later.

In all of these areas (and of course these are just a selection) I hope you can see how useful it is likely to be for you to have some dedicated preparation time when you investigate in order to clarify or inform your later studies.

Preparatory and preliminary kinds of studies

At this point I fear I may be accused of being pedantic when I suggest that there is a difference between preparatory investigations such as in the areas exemplified above and investigations that are more truly 'preliminary'. Here I am taking a preliminary study to mean one that is the first in a series and which precedes the major studies and has a place in that series. The reporting of such a study would necessarily be included in a final submission because it is a necessary part of the overall programme that has led to the outcomes you are submitting for assessment. In other words, the assessors need to see the preliminary studies in order to understand the major ones. In contrast, the assessors would not necessarily need to see preparatory studies because they are not necessary to an understanding of the whole. Perhaps an example that might shed light on my interpretation here is where a 'preliminary' sketch of a landscape by an artist might be a work that is worthy of appreciation in its own right (though it may be small scale, unfinished and lacking in some colour and some detail), whereas 'preparation' might involve (merely) testing out colours from a palette and brushes from a selection or indeed visits to a location at different times of the day and in different weathers.

Whether or not you agree with my distinction, my point is to draw your attention to two purposes within this opening phase of research work: first, the preparing of the practical and intellectual tools that you will use in your substantive investigations, and second, some initial (preliminary) investigation that acts as a precursor to substantive ones.

Suggestions for further reading

Section 1 of Further Reading contains publications that refer to many of the issues tackled in this chapter particularly in respect of the preparatory and preliminary phases of your research work.

Narrowing down a topic

You might think that narrowing down a topic or focusing, as it might better be expressed, could well have been included in the above section on preparation as it is a part of the initial stages of preparing to investigate – and you would be right. Yet I have chosen to separate it out here for special consideration because it is so crucial and, again, it is an aspect of research degree study that marks the latter out as distinctive.

Research degree students often enter the arena of research degree study with ideas of what to investigate that are rooted in their previous experience of academic work (often at masters level), or professional or personal interest or a combination of all these things. While ambitions to research into topics that are dear to the heart and to which you are intellectually wedded are, in one sense, laudable, those ambitions may need to be tempered by the realism of what is achievable within the time and the resources available and what is intellectually an answerable and worthwhile set of research questions. A significant element within the planning of a research degree programme is therefore very often narrowing down a topic from a broad interest to a manageable research project (in both pragmatic and intellectual senses) that is appropriate for the kind and level of research degree award that is the target of the study.

I give below some examples of processes that such narrowing down may involve, and again I am doing this as an indication of the kinds of things that are involved rather than with any intention of providing an exhaustive and all-inclusive list (such a list would not be relevant across all disciplines):

- Specifying a target group of subjects or phenomena from within a broad range (e.g. choosing to study the effects of melting ice caps on the breeding patterns of Emperor Penguins rather than in relation to all penguins).
- Discounting some variables by focusing on a selected few (e.g. looking at excessively low temperatures as a specific factor in engine wear – rather than looking at engine wear more generally at differing temperatures).
- Taking a specific time frame that is narrower than initially intended (e.g. looking at army desertion rates within the last few weeks of the First World War rather than desertion rates throughout that war).
- Choosing to analyse data using a selected approach(es) rather than using a whole range of approaches (e.g. using interviews only to investigate nurses' attitudes to self-injuring patients rather than including questionnaires and observations).

In all the kinds of dimensions exemplified above the research student needs to operate upon some rational basis when making decisions and that rationality needs to be made explicit. Examiners are quite entitled to question you on why you chose to focus your work in the way that you did. They may require you to justify your decisions in any of the examples given above. The rationale for your studies will need to contain justification for why some things were omitted, or rather selected out, as a result of your process of focusing.

One significant aspect of any such justification would be an acknowledgement of the effects on your overall conclusions of the choices you made and an illustration of the benefits accruing from the focusing that warrant the loss of other possible conclusions. For example, in the instance of using interviews with nurses above, quite clearly what you would get by way of results would be the nurses' views of their own attitudes and the results would not necessarily reflect on how they behave towards the self-injuring patients and thus how those supposed attitudes are manifest. It is for you and your supervisory team to weigh up the advantages of the focus and the disadvantages of its limitations as you plan your research programme. It is often a matter of fine intellectual judgement as to the balance between advantage and disadvantage, between a research study that is worthwhile despite its limitations and a study that is irreparably flawed because of those limitations. Whatever the case, you do need to recognize that all research degree programmes of study are defined by their limits. There is only so much time and there is only so much resource available; it is for you and your supervisors to ensure that the limits you work within are understood, reasonable and defensible to your assessors in terms of the coherence of the findings.

Phasing the development of the project

Some projects lend themselves to phasing and some are less readily amenable to it. So, a project where different levels of experiment need to be carried out in a sequential way in order to reach the required kinds of conclusion may well, naturally, fall into discrete though connected parts that are easy to describe in a phased way. For example, many projects within the natural sciences are of this type. Yet there are other projects where the progress through a research plan is a relatively seamless business and where breaking the whole down into component parts may be more difficult.

Wherever your particular project falls along the continuum from phased to non-phased you may still be required to set out how your work will progress through the proposed period of time of a research programme. You may then need to describe work to be carried out in the first year, then the second year, and so on. If your university requires you to set out phases of the project in advance of your actual investigatory work then you need to understand their purpose in so doing. What institutions are afraid of (on your behalf as well as their own) is that programmes of study will drift and may enter stages of limbo where little is achieved. Increasingly, universities are required to monitor more closely what their research students are doing and to do this they need some clarity set out at the start about what is to be done. What you need to do therefore is to begin to conceive of your project as requiring of you chunks of time and commitment. You should be able to break down what you will be doing over, say, a three year time frame of study even if it means setting targets for the production of parts of the (seamless) whole. If you have experience of marking out projects in these terms within your own professional background or workplace context, then that may come in very useful here.

Task: reflecting on phasing within your workplace (professional) background

- Are there examples from your working context outside of academia where you have been required, formally or informally, to plan work in phases or stages or across particular points of reference?
- If so, are there any lessons to be learned from such examples that might inform your planning within the context of your research degree studies?
- Similarly, do you have particular (professional) planning skills that may be brought to bear on planning your programme of research studies?

Pretty well everything we do is planned in phases. Time is allocated for development and agreement then for the build itself. In fact, a key skill for us is to get the project management right so that nobody is left waiting for somebody else and one thing follows another with minimal delays. That's what clients expect. Basic materials, work, fittings and finishes it all has to come together. My bit in all this is the design but I have to think about all that follows and advise the project managers about contingencies and so on. So, yes I think I can bring a lot of practical planning skills to my studies. But I still feel uneasy because, while I am familiar with planning for a build, all this academic study is very different . . . and I am not so sure . . . what would count as a sensible contingency for example . . . I'll have to think about that.

(Architect registered for a professional doctorate)

Whatever the level of difficulty you may have in predicting phases to be gone through in your research there are distinct advantages for you in doing so (as well as the need to meet university requirements). Breaking down a large and complex set of tasks into linked elements may make the daunting seem more approachable and the large and amorphous more local and definable. It may help you to manage your work more carefully. Of course, you must strive not to lose sight of the whole of the research enterprise by focusing on its constituent parts and on the immediate.

Task: phasing your research work

- Take the whole of your proposed research project and try to see how it may be described as falling into distinct phases or stages or time periods.
- Use diagrams or charts (e.g. a Gantt chart) or list of words in sections and subsections as appropriate to your study. Don't worry about overlapping parts of the work and don't fret unduly if what you have set down seems an artificial imposition – it may have value nonetheless.
- How achievable are the discrete parts within the overall time frame available?

> **Suggestions for further reading**
> Section 2 of Further Reading contains texts that refer to issues of phasing, for example Bell (2005) and Rugg and Petre (2006).

Getting started

As noted earlier, getting started on research is sometimes a matter of plunging in and carrying out an investigation. On the other hand, sometimes it is a matter of planning in detail what you will do and when; this may apply particularly when you are working in collaboration with a number of others on a project or on linked projects within a larger whole. This is a matter for you and your supervisors to decide and the judgement depends on the project and its disciplinary context and so on. I have set out some examples of ideas that may help. Please note that not all of these will apply to you, indeed I have deliberately set down some that are contrary to each other to indicate that there are always choices to be made. The beauty of research degree study is that it requires that *you* make them.

- Try to spot when you are prevaricating – if you think that you are then try to find the reasons why and this may help you to find a way to break what can often be a downward spiral of prevarication, delay, justification for further delay and further prevarication.
- Get on with some practical investigation, however exploratory and preparatory that may be.
- Write down an outline of your research programme in a linear fashion and flesh out as much detail as you can predict at this stage (and do not hold yourself to it later – though you may wish to refer to it to keep a hold on what you end up doing and not doing and why).
- Draw a diagram (that may well accommodate to the non-linear) that covers what you intend to achieve in your research studies and find the place where it is logical to begin – start there.
- Revisit the core aim of what you thought you were trying to 'find out' and see if it is still appropriate and if not try to decide why not and how it needs to be amended. Try to think backwards from the ultimate research goal, which you now think you are now working towards, to where you are now and hence plot some kind of pathway from your present state to that goal.

Summary

- You have been asked to consider what is distinctive in the planning stage of a research degree and in particular have been encouraged to understand your part in that process.
- You have considered what needs to be done by way of preparing for the research work that is to develop through the course of research degree programme.
- You have been given some notion of the various pitfalls and possible delays that may occur in this stage of your research work and have been given some ideas about how to avoid those pitfalls and deal with those delays.

Conclusion

Preparation is all important at research degree level in part at least because, yet again, there is no existing curriculum for you to follow and hence in preparing for your studies you need to carefully refine ideas and adopt methods and approaches until they are both doable and likely to yield research results that are appropriate to satisfy the level of award for which you are intending to submit. Above all else, in your individual programme of studies you will be learning about research by doing research and it is perhaps important to note that all research involves careful preparation if it is not to be wasteful in terms of time and energy. You need therefore to learn about research preparation as part of the required knowledge of a researcher and, in collaboration with your supervisors, you need to make sure that the particular project that is to form the basis for your learning about research is (within the terms of your discipline) reasonable, intellectually coherent and ethical.

While research may well be conceived of as going up alleys to see if they are blind, as Marston Bates suggests, you would be unwise to go up too many blind alleys or indeed to find yourself trapped in one.

7

Effective reading and listening

> *The greatest part of a writer's time is spent in reading, in order to write; a man will turn over half a library to make one book.*
>
> Samuel Johnson (1709–1784), taken from Boswell's
> *Life of Johnson* (1791)

Overview

This chapter deals with accessing information and ideas, be it from books or from speakers or from observations of other researchers in operation (or indeed from professionals making use of research knowledge, techniques or published findings in their practice). In this chapter, therefore, you will be asked to:

- consider how to choose what to read as well as how to make the process of reading more efficient in terms of your own learning and researching
- explore different kinds of information sources and their relative usefulness in your studying and researching

- think about ways of using your note taking as an effective learning strategy
- evaluate the importance of developing a bank of references and a system for dealing with ideas as they arise during the development of your research project.

Introduction

Samuel Johnson may not have had research degree students in mind when he talked of the 'greater part of a writer's time' (see quote above). But the notion that to produce worthwhile text requires input in the form of reading holds true in today's research world just as it did in the eighteenth century. As someone who is returning to study you may think that you know enough to write a research proposal or report without worrying too much about the troublesome business of reading, but I suggest that such a notion would be deceptive. Research degree study demands that you as a student 'read' for your academic award just as you would expect to for any other university degree.

In your own programme of research study you may not have the opportunity to go regularly to lectures and seminars, though it is likely that you will listen to someone talking about academic matters in tutorial settings and attend research conferences and seminars. But wherever the opportunity exists it needs to be exploited. And while listening may seem an everyday and hence unremarkable event it requires skill if it is to be utilized effectively in the context of learning at an advanced level about how to do research.

Suggestions for further reading

You may wish to complement your reading of this chapter by referring to some of the texts listed in Section 3 of Further Reading.

Effective reading

Reading lists and key journals

If you were registered for a taught degree course, you could expect to be provided with lists of introductory or core reading which encompass basic concepts and ideas and give suggestions for further reading to clarify particular issues. As you will guess, such an approach is not amenable to research degree study. At the outset of your studies your supervisory team may well recommend some key texts and these are as likely to be seminal or current research papers as they are to be books, but your supervisors' recommendations are most probably conceived of as starting points where you may explore ideas for yourself rather than as set texts that are effectively required reading.

In short, you are returning to study at a higher level than your past experience of academic life and therefore it is important to note that while reading from set texts and regurgitating specific information in an acceptable form may be seen as desirable at some academic levels, it is not appropriate at research degree level. That is not to say that some parts of your final submission may not contain a restating of certain information that is already in the public or academic domain, indeed some restating of this kind is almost inevitable. But the purpose now is different in that you are not setting down facts and figures to demonstrate that you have learned a body of knowledge and mastered some intellectual and practical skills. Your purpose is more likely to revolve around the need to clarify the intellectual territory within which you intend to develop your argument, based on research findings. For the purposes of this chapter, this requires that you read in order to understand issues and to clarify your own ideas about how to push back the boundaries of the known to include the new insights that you will develop through carrying out investigations. You are not merely accumulating more personal knowledge for the sake of 'knowing more'.

Task: your area of research study
- Is your chosen area of research study relatively new or has it been established over a period of time?
- What are the implications of this for you as a researcher and as a learner about research?

People have been researching into medical technologies in one sense or another since the start of recorded history, but in recent years there has been a huge leap forward in general and certainly in my own field; in my case brought about in the main by the introduction of robotics into surgery. It's been amazing.

(MD student)

Relatively old, still loads written on it, no real implementations – all research builds on what's gone on before whether 'new' or established. All existing knowledge is open to challenge which makes it difficult sometimes for me as a student to draw conclusions.

(Nurse enrolled for an MSc by research)

Almost completely new in specific terms, there is no 'one' journal from which to get relevant information, it is difficult to tease out pieces which are salient.

(Government lawyer registered for a PhD)

Narrowing down your reading

It is, as ever, important to narrow down your reading and here your supervisors should be able to help, but I would suggest that in seeking such guidance you try to be clear about the question you are asking. In my view, you should not expect your supervisor to do your thinking, or indeed searching, for you. Rather, you need to ask to be pointed in the right direction. To ask for guidance effectively therefore, you do need to have thought about the purpose behind your reading. To ask 'What should I be reading?' is a question that is too broad; at the very least you need to qualify that with '. . . in order to find out about x?' In your research degree study you need to become an expert on both what is known and what is being discovered; it would not be unusual therefore for your supervisor to begin, quite quickly in your registration, to look to you to tell him or her about new developments in respect of your particular project. In this sense supervisors may quite legitimately develop an expectation that you keep them abreast of the latest developments, not vice versa.

Suggestions for further reading

If your research is within the social sciences then you might find it helpful at this point to refer to Bell (2005) or Denscombe (2007); see Section 2 of Further Reading.

Reading research texts

Some of my research students in the past have benefited from structuring their own reading by using a set of questions that enable them to focus on the relevance and usefulness of texts as well as challenge what is being said and the way in which it is expressed. I give some examples below, again not with an intention of offering an exhaustive list but rather some indications of the kinds of approach you might take.

- What is the crux of the message that the researcher is trying to get across in this paper?
- Is there any tension between the research methods the researcher has reportedly used and the kinds of conclusions he or she is making?
- How can I adopt or adapt this methodology or research finding in developing my own research project?
- Does the evidence provided by the research findings justify the claims

that the writer is making (e.g. the implications for professional practice or further research)?

Some of these students formalized this procedure into a set list of self-checking questions that they came to use every time they read a paper. While this may seem cumbersome, and perhaps even restrictive, they have indicated to me that their method did enable them to focus and to do so in a consistently critical way.

I leave it to you to decide how far to take the use of self-checking questions but, whatever strategy you employ, your reading of research articles and books should be not only about understanding what results or findings have been presented, but also about working out the following:

- What ideas are the driving force behind the text.
- How the researcher comes to choose what to put into the text and what to leave out.
- How the researcher comes to choose the particular style of presentation used in the paper or book.
- Whether or not the researcher's assumptions and conclusions are realistic in terms of your own experience of the research field in question.
- The directions and further problems that arise from the research that is reported in the writing and, if they are relevant to your own (intended) research, whether or not they are resolvable by you within the context of your own research degree study.
- Any patterns (of difficulty, kind of research question being asked or research method(s) being employed) that are becoming apparent to you as you extend your reading of the literature within the research area.

The point is, of course, that you need to see reading the research literature as more than just a way of gaining information. It is also an opportunity to learn about how to interpret research findings and events and phenomena within your own intellectual experience and how to write in a style that is acceptable within your particular research area (there are some universals of style but also variations between areas).

Checking against previously submitted work

When you come to write your submission for a research degree award (be it a dissertation or a thesis) then it is important that you check out what kind of thing has been successful in the past and specifically at your level (e.g. doctoral or research masters) and within your discipline. Most university libraries will hold dissertations and theses submitted successfully for research degrees and these can usually, though not always, be viewed fairly easily. Clearly, you have to be careful in making judgements when looking through old research dissertations and theses because you will not know necessarily which of the collection were exceptionally good and which just managed a pass (and, though it may not be widely acknowledged, there is such a distinction even at doctoral level). Even when writing a minor research report or upgrade document it may well be helpful for you as a returning research degree student to look at samples of work that have been successfully submitted in your university at the level at which you are currently studying and for the particular purpose that is relevant (e.g. upgrade or progression documents often have a specified and perhaps idiosyncratic appearance and format). The same caveats about level of success of previous work still apply; nevertheless looking at a range of previously submitted work (if that can be made available) will give you a feel for kinds of expectation.

The primary purpose, then, of looking at previously submitted research work is for you to begin to judge the kind of quality that is required at the level you have entered and to begin to gauge expectations of assessors in terms of quantity (e.g. number of words allowed) and kind of presentation (e.g. use of devices such as diagrammatic representations, style of referencing of previous research, accepted conventions of prose) as well as the more formal and discipline specific issues such as how to report methods used and how to present complex analyses and subsequent research findings. In many discipline areas it is also useful to begin to get a feel for the range of studies that fall within any one disciplinary area. You may well find that when you return to study after some years away from it, the 'subject' that you thought you knew has changed direction or expanded or become inextricably linked to other, previously distinct, areas of intellectual concern and research inquiry. Again, interdisciplinarity has increasingly become a feature both of professional work and of research endeavour both within the boundaries of academia and outside of it. Often research degree programmes reflect this increasing concern to see the links between disciplines and between research fields. Looking at current, submitted research degree work enables you to orientate yourself to the concerns, limits, methodologies and connections of your own and related discipline and research areas.

Making and using notes as a tool for developing research

Your own use of notes

Notes are made and used in research as a matter of common practice; however, they also feature in the world outside of formal research and academia in a number of guises and in order to fulfil a number of purposes. In this respect it may be useful for you to recall your own experiences (see 'Task: your own use of notes' below).

> **Task: your own use of notes**
> - If you have made notes in the past (either in previous academic study or in any professional background that you may have), have you done so with a conscious intention of using them again in the future?
> - Have you made as much use of your notes as you thought you would at the time of making them (and if not why not)?
> - Have there been distinctions between the kinds of notes you have made in any professional work that you have undertaken (or in any personal situation) as opposed to those made during your previous experience of academic study?
> - What are the implications of any such distinctions for future note taking?

My note taking has been deliberate: sometimes through habit, sometimes to keep focused, sometimes to sort thoughts out when reading.

> (Education consultant embarking on an EdD)

When I was an undergraduate student, years and years ago now, I would write everything down blindly, hoping it would come in useful later. In my medical work I tend to be much more choosey and I only note down what I need to refer to later. I guess I am much more selective than when I was an undergraduate. But in my medical work of course I tend to know what I am looking for and I know what I need to record and what I will use it for later.

> (MD student)

Professional notes are legal documents. Academic notes used for study can be rough.

> (Midwife at the mid-point of an MSc by research)

If it seems that notes have not been particularly useful to you, then clearly you need to reconsider how their effectiveness can be improved for you now as a research student, or indeed if taking notes is worth the effort in the first place. If there are distinctions between the way in which you have used note taking in your personal or professional life as opposed to in your academic work in the past then it may be worth considering why those differences have arisen and why one form of usage has proved more profitable for you than the other.

Taking notes during reading

It may be that summarizing what you have read in research journals and so on is most useful to you if it is in the form of written notes which précis the original in continuous prose. In my view, however, it is more likely that the meaning of the text in front of you will be more accessible in future if the prose is broken up into headed subsections in that subheadings allow you to find your way around your notes at a later date. Indeed it may be that breaking down your notes into single words and phrases is most effective both in terms of ease of recording and subsequent memory prompting. This kind of skeleton outline of what is presented in the text is probably the most popular form of note taking. Headings and subheadings then become the significant tool for summarizing text; they also become a significant aspect of the way in which you rework the meaning in your head and make sense of it for yourself.

An alternative to the methods suggested above is to develop a system for yourself in which you produce notes in a more diagrammatic format. Here the study skills terminology varies from 'patterned notes' to 'spray diagram' to 'spider charts'. While the focus is still on you setting down the key words as you understand them, you write the main issue or concept centrally on the page and connect subsequent key words to that central issue with lines. When points are made by the writer (or indeed by a speaker) which are connected to these subsequent words then you can attach them accordingly (i.e. to the peripheral words rather than directly to the centre) thus forming clusters around the periphery of the page. An example is shown in Figure 7.1.

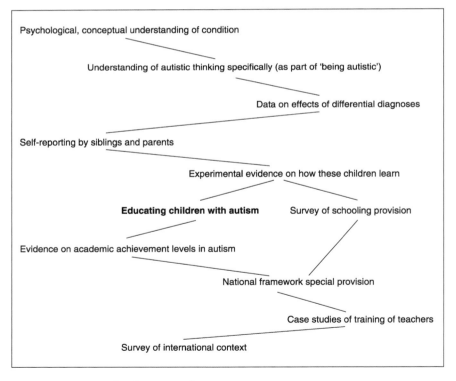

Figure 7.1 Example of patterned notes

Importantly, the resulting spider's web of key concepts and connecting lines of evidence and argument should enable you to develop an understanding not only of the key issues but also of the way in which those issues are connected (by the researcher if not in the real world of your own experience). The advantage of this kind of system is therefore that it enables you both to record what is being said or written and to construct your own related framework of meaning at the same time. There are clearly a number of variations on the basic spider diagram described above. Clusters can be connected to other clusters, arrows on lines can be used to indicate the direction of evidence or argument, connecting lines can be given more or less importance, comments can be written later to elaborate on your own understanding of (and challenge to) the researcher's written or oral expression of ideas and findings. Also, you may choose to make a linear set of notes in the first instance and then later transform them into a more diagrammatic format; in this way you may come to see connections in a presentation of research (or perhaps disconnections) which were not immediately apparent as you listened or read.

Developing a bank of references

Working towards a substantial piece of work such as a thesis or dissertation that may involve, for example, a series of research studies requires that you pay particular attention to the need for a structured way of recording what you read. Obviously, when a research author cites something that looks interesting, you need to make a note of it somehow if it is to be retrievable later – assuming you will remember is folly. Therefore, early on in your research studies you need to establish a bank of useful references and develop an effective system of cross-referencing that will enable you to find what you want without undue waste of time as you progress through what is probably the longest and most complex piece of work you have ever encountered.

The initial difficulty for you is in creating the kinds of categories that will sustain your particular research work as it progresses. It is worth spending some time in developing a flexible yet robust system of cross-referencing based perhaps on the kinds of concern that are at the root of your developing thesis or, if you are engaged in research work that is related to your professional practice, then based on a structure that relates to your professional life. Whatever you start with will almost certainly need to be developed but as long as you have actually started then developments are possible. An example of how you might proceed is given in 'Task: developing a bank of references'.

Task: developing a bank of references

Try to follow this outline procedure:

- Set down in note form what you require from a bank of references that will enable your research work to develop.

- Experiment with some categories that might form the basis of a cross-referencing system.
- Test out your system with some specific examples.
- Evaluate and modify.
- Re-test with some new examples.

I spent quite a long time on this task partly because I got it pretty wrong the first time. My project is on oriental ceramics and I decided to combine notes with references. I started one section on 'notes that aid identification' (of ceramic pieces) and a separate one which was effectively a dictionary of sources of meanings and other information. I didn't bother with the testing bit because I thought it would work and so I started to use it. But the notes on identification section simply did not work (the categories kept overlapping) and after a while I abandoned that and focused on sorting out what I called my dictionary, which then included the other 'notes'. This is now working well and, though it takes time to keep it up to date, I can see that it will be invaluable later.

(Museum archivist working on a PhD about Chinese funerary ceramics of the Ming period)

Suggestions for further reading
In terms of some of the broader issues relating to 'making use of notes' you will find help in the books listed in Section 8 of Further Reading (e.g. Northedge 1990).

Listening to what is happening in professional practice as a tool to developing a research awareness

It would be remiss of me to ignore professional practice as a potential source of research information and ideas. If you are engaged in research that relates to, or is rooted in, your own professional practice, then you need to develop ways of becoming aware of the current issues that are engaging your professional colleagues and impacting on the users, clients or recipients of your profession. As someone learning about research you need to begin to see your professional work as the place where you engage in learning (about research as well as about the profession) and the source of the dynamic that sparks off new avenues of research question and that may hold the potential to resolve previously recognized but unresolved issues. If a problem arises in your professional practice that is not readily resolvable with existing methods, strategies or resources then you need to ask yourself about the aspects of the underlying issue that are making it problematic. Some examples of such self-questioning are given below.

- What is the underlying issue?
- Why is it not readily resolvable?
- What do potential resolutions require if they are to be effective?
- Can investigation of any kind help in achieving a resolution?
- Do the questions/investigation impinge in any way upon my own planned research programme?

As you develop in your professional practice as a practitioner who is familiar with research methodologies and potentials and who uses research proactively in your own developing practice then learning to listen and observe from the perspective of a researcher (rather than as 'just' a professional) is crucial to your ongoing success. Studying for a research degree should mean that there is value added to you as a professional. Indeed, it is arguable that you should aim to become a different kind of professional, one for whom researching and (professional) practising become intertwined and interdependent. Each aspect of your overall approach to your work informs the other until, ideally, the aspects become indistinguishable.

Summary

- You have considered strategies for making your reading about research more efficient.
- You have thought about your existing style of note taking and have reflected on strategies for developing it.
- You have considered developing a bank of references and experimenting with a system of cross-referencing.
- You have considered ways of listening and observing within any relevant professional context so as to develop yourself, where appropriate, as a researcher or practitioner.

Conclusion

'Turning over half a library' (see the quotation from Johnson at the start of the chapter) may seem a little excessive, especially when we consider the size of many current university libraries. However, it does help to recognize that reading is an essential prerequisite to investigating or indeed setting pen to paper to produce writing that can qualify for a research degree. Therefore the question that this chapter should have left you with is: 'How best can I structure my reading and my note taking so as to get the most out of my subsequent writing about my research?' If your research work is based within your professional practice then a subsidiary question for you as a professional is: 'Does reading for research purposes differ in any meaningful way from the kind of reading I do in my professional life?' Clearly, the answer to this latter question will affect the kinds of structures and strategies you choose to adopt and develop.

8

Effective writing about your research

Overview • Introduction • Writing as part of the process of studying and researching • The early stages in academic writing about research • Developing a structure for reporting your research • Some conventions in academic writing about research • Writing about research within a professional context • Using your reading • Referencing • Summary • Conclusion

> *Writing, when properly managed (as you can imagine I think mine is) is but a different name for conversation.*
>
> Laurence Sterne (1713–1768), *Tristram Shandy,*
> Book 2, Chapter 11 (1759)

Overview

This chapter deals with the stage at which you engage in planning your writing about your research. In this chapter, therefore, you will be asked to:

- consider the preparatory and initial stages of producing written work, in terms of how you may conceive of the process of writing about your research as an inextricable part of the overall process of studying and of developing your research degree programme

- think about some of the problems you may face in getting started on producing written work
- contemplate how you may choose to structure your written work for your readers and use the process of structuring as a part of your overall strategy for effective writing
- consider some of the purposes of writing in academic study about research and points of technique and convention
- think about the interface between any professional experience you may have and the production of research reports and dissertations
- reflect on the way in which your reading of academic texts (and professional texts where appropriate) needs to feed into your written work.

Introduction

It may seem enticing for you, as someone returning to study at research degree level, to focus your attention on the act of writing and to see this aspect of your study as all important. But it is probably a mistake to assume that 'If only I could write well I could achieve my research degree'. Certainly, a weak argument can be made to sound stronger by a judicious use of prose but it will remain a weak argument nonetheless. What is required of you is that you focus, in the first instance at least, on what the message (or material or set of data) is that you wish to convey to your reader. The stage of planning to write is, therefore, all important.

As has been noted in earlier chapters the whole purpose of academic writing is to convey meaning clearly and succinctly. It seems to me, therefore, that a reasonable model to have in your mind would be that when you write you are engaging in a kind of conversation with your audience, as Laurence Sterne implies in the quote at the start of this chapter. It is, however, a conversation in which you cannot modulate your pace or your direction in the light of the things that your conversational partner says – you get no immediate feedback. Effective writing therefore requires that you be particularly considerate of your audience's (your conversational partner's) needs.

Writing as part of the process of studying and researching

You may have encountered a 'traditional' view of writing in academic research work that suggests that it is something that takes place after content has been decided upon and after the thinking and the investigating has taken place. In short, you do your thinking, reading and investigating and then you write it up. Indeed, this interpretation is reified within many institutional structures where periods of study time are demarcated as 'writing-up periods'. My own view is that this interpretation is misleading in that the process of developing ideas and the act of writing them down as text should not be conceived of as separate and distinct activities. To me, the business of writing is better conceived of as being inextricably linked with the process of thinking. I suggest to you that you may find that setting down text forces you to clarify what you mean. Finding ways of expressing your research ideas is, in part at least, a process of formulating those ideas or at least developing them further. This view is well expressed by Torrance and Thomas (1994); see Section 3 of Further Reading.

When planning to write I suggest that it is necessary to unravel just what the purpose of the writing is to be for you. It follows that you can conceive of it as the business of expressing ideas for the consumption of the eventual assessor, while you may also take a more formative approach and interpret your writing as part of the development of your own ideas. Whatever the rights or wrongs of the differing interpretations I outline above, you need to start the process of writing (albeit in rough form) earlier rather than later in the overall process of your research degree programme.

The early stages in academic writing about research

Suggestions for further reading

I have been influenced in my writing of this section by a number of texts that are listed in Section 3 of Further Reading and you may find it helpful to refer to them here, in particular Weissberg and Buker (1990).

Deciding on content

As a returning student you may feel somewhat overwhelmed by the task of writing for a particular audience in a particular style within a particular word length etc. All of these things are important of course (and indeed they are dealt with in this chapter) but the primary concern is that you have something to say and that you know what it is. Often what seems to be a problem of setting down words that make sense (i.e. what seems to be a problem in the mechanics of writing) is really a problem of not knowing what it is that you want to say. You may find that you need to take time out to think through what your content is to be and then go about setting it down as simply and directly as you can. Again, experience has shown that a common misconception in the early stages of returning to study is to assume that one of the purposes of academic writing is to sound clever. In fact the prime purpose is to convey meaning clearly, precisely and simply.

Setting the scene for the reader

In any piece of written work, it is important that you set the scene for your reader so that as they begin to read your text they have the forthcoming content organized for them. A direct way for you to do this is to include a short abstract or introduction which summarizes what your paper is about. This device is commonplace in the world of academic research, indeed it will almost certainly be a compulsory part of any final submission for a research degree (i.e. there is likely to be a formal requirement for an abstract, usually with a defined word length). But there is nothing to stop you using the same method of scene setting in any written work that forms part of your research degree programme, e.g. in research reports, articles for publication, progress or upgrade reports and so on.

Where you have carried out any investigation that you need to report for whatever purpose then you need to summarize for your reader what was done, what was found and very briefly what the major implications are. I accept, of course, that to achieve this in one short paragraph is not an easy matter, but this does not lessen its importance. The use of abstracts in this respect is revisited in Chapter 9.

Similarly, you should not be afraid to summarize content of any research writing at the outset in diagrammatic form if that is appropriate. For example, a time-line might be helpful to your reader if the research being described reports events over a period, a map may be helpful if the research problem is spatial, a 'family tree' may summarize complex relationships that were explored in the research investigation, and so on.

Adopting the right tone

In part, finding the appropriate tone for a paper is a matter of adopting the conventions of academic research writing (which are tackled later in this chapter) but it is also a matter of adapting to the particular culture within which you are writing. I am using the term 'culture' here to encompass both macro (in my case academia in, initially, the UK) and the micro (the specific culture of the research discipline concerned). For example, in the UK, research findings tend to be written up in a non-assertive way and in the sciences tend to revolve around evidence and proof. Within this kind of culture you would be unwise to try to 'sell' your work (as being, for example, startlingly innovative or offering genuine insights) or to neglect a rigorous analysis of what counts as evidence.

Also, you should bear in mind that you are writing for a human audience.

Certainly, your argument needs to be rational and any conclusions 'correct' if you are to achieve the research degree that is your aim but the reporting of your work has to be easy to read and understand. A common difficulty experienced by research students, and indeed perhaps by researchers in general, is to rely too much on the reader doing some of the work for them. When writing about your research you should not expect your reader to make deductions regarding what you mean in your text nor should you expect them to see through oblique statements and recognize the implications of what you have written. I can think of many occasions where in discussing writing about research with a student I have ended up commenting, 'but you haven't said that'; sometimes this is followed by protestations from the student, 'but I meant that'. The point is of course that, as the reader, I know only what I have in front of me. The problem for you as a writer about your research is that while you may be immersed in your topic, it is helpful to acknowledge in the tone you adopt that your reader will not necessarily be so involved. You need, therefore, to point out clearly all that the reader needs to know to understand what you did in your research and what you found and what it means without, of course, labouring the obvious points. Clearly, one way to do this is to put yourself in the place of the reader and try to see from their perspective what it is that he or she needs to know in order to make sense of the text.

Blocks to writing

At some point in your programme of research degree study you may find it difficult to make progress with your writing. The term 'writer's block' is often used in this kind of circumstance; this at least gives the impression that what you are suffering from is some common condition that is identifiable and therefore holds out the possibility of remediation at least or cure at best. In fact of course there is no such thing as writer's block per se. However, there is a set of problems that commonly afflict those engaged in the process of writing and Table 8.1 on 'Blocks to writing' offers some common reasons why progress in writing may seem unattainable at certain points and offers some possible solutions in the form of comments.

Developing a structure for reporting your research

General purpose of outlines

In my view you would be advised to construct an outline *before* you start to write about your research because then you will be able to see more readily whether or not there is a sense of logic and balance in the way in which you intend to set out your reporting of your work. This sense can be achieved in

Table 8.1 Blocks to writing

Problem	Comment
'Whenever I start to write the words simply do not seem to be good enough'	You need to see writing as a process in which your ideas about your research may change as you write; what you write at the start does not have to be the final product – word processors have made it ever more possible to write something inadequate at first and return to it later to make it right. Perfection of writing is unlikely in any case, but it is unrealistic to expect it at the first effort. What is needed is to start putting down some of the key ideas about your research (without worrying unduly about form) and using the process of writing to clarify those ideas and so in turn enable an easier flow of writing.
'I have a hopeless feeling that writing any kind of worthwhile text is beyond my immediate scope.'	Consider starting by setting down an outline (see the section in this chapter on using an outline) of what you intend to convey in the piece of research reporting upon which you are engaged; then work from the broad outline towards finer detail until you have some sense of a specific subsection that can be begun.
'I assume that the writing about my research can and should be written from start to finish in sequential order and I am uncertain about what the starting point should be. My research is simply not linear like that.'	Again, think about starting simply by writing down the key ideas that you want to put across. Then go back and think about writing the introduction (having clarified in your own mind what the research project is about in essence) or perhaps one of the later sections – just because a research paper or indeed final submission may be read from start to finish does not mean that it has to be written in that order.

different ways as will become apparent in the sections that follow, but whatever method is employed your reader needs to feel that there is some reason and deliberate purpose about the way the text is set out. An outline which gives headings and subheadings can reveal to you in this preparatory stage how your content is balanced and how clearly the various parts of your writing support a developing and coherent argument or description. If the research that you are reporting develops from a specified research question through various arguments, or the presentation of different kinds of empirical evidence, and then returns full circle to the original question then you need to make clear in the outline that this 'circularity' is deliberate and subsequently you need to make this overt in the text.

Some alternative ways of structuring written work

At the planning stage it is worth considering different ways of structuring any written reporting of research (see Table 8.2 on 'Approaches to developing an outline structure for reporting on research'). Again no one way has universal superiority, it is a matter of choosing a kind of structure that is amenable to the particular piece of reporting that faces you and is appropriate to your discipline; neither are the ways suggested in Table 8.2 mutually exclusive, indeed there is clear overlap. The notion of going from the general to the specific and back to the general, which is adapted below, is described by Dane (1990) in the book *Research Methods* using the analogy of an hour-glass; the notion of considering structure from the perspective of the writer is adapted from Sides (1992) *How to Write and Present Technical Information.*

A common feature of the approaches given in Table 8.2 is the suggestion that it might be useful for you to revisit early parts of a paper or submission later in the light of research findings. While the usefulness may seem specific to a scientific paradigm (as in the first of the examples in Table 8.2) it is, in fact, generally useful to think of revisiting the early parts of a research study or the initial research question in the discussion and conclusion. After all the reader needs to see how you have made sense of what you have discovered or unravelled through your research. In my own view, closing the circle is a useful device in reporting research regardless of discipline and is something that can be planned for in the initial stages of planning to write about your research, in whatever context that falls.

The books by Dane (1990) and Sides (1992) address the issue of structure explicitly and would make useful supplementary reading to this section.

Building a structure around questions

In some subject areas and for specific kinds of research reporting it may be particularly helpful if you can structure your work around key research questions (a simple example might be to use subheadings in question form such as 'What evidence is there that the *x* financial market has declined?' rather than 'The decline of the *x* financial market'). The advantage of this approach is that it may force you to sharpen up the reporting of your research into a critical argument rather than leave it as a collection of pieces of evidence, information and ultimately opinion. However, the disadvantage may be that the use of questions will lead your reader to expect some answers from you and therefore you do need to deliver (or explain why *an* answer is not, in your view, possible or desirable within the constraints of your particular research programme). If you decide to use a series of questions then clearly they should build one upon the other or at least be related one to another.

Table 8.2 Approaches to developing an outline structure for reporting on research

---

From the general to the specific and back to the general
- Introduce the general context of the research that you are reporting; describe any particular theoretical framework necessary for an understanding of what is to follow; give any empirical context of the research and any specific hypotheses that are to be tested.
- Describe any participants, materials and procedures in a 'methods' section.
- Cite any data and offer analyses in a 'results' section.
- Discuss how the results relate to the hypotheses, reconsider the empirical and theoretical contexts in terms of the analyses of the data.
- Return full circle to the general context and, again, reconsider in the light of overall findings.

Note that this approach can be rewritten in a less scientific way. For example: describe the general context of the research question (e.g. comic characters in Shakespeare's plays), discuss the specific research question that is to be explored (e.g. what is the evidence for understanding the kinds of function they were intended to fulfil), analyse an exemplar (e.g. contemporaneous notes relating to the functions fulfilled by the character of the Porter in *Macbeth*). You would then return from the specific to the general (to take the same example: by relating the analysis of the comic character(s) in *Macbeth* to those in the other main tragedies, making reference of the relationship you thus define within the tragedies to the rest of the Shakespearean canon, perhaps drawing a comparison with contemporary writings about the use of comic characters in Elizabethan drama in general (this last stage actually goes beyond your original starting point in terms of generality)).

Problem solving
- Give the context within which the research problem state exists.
- Describe that problem state, indicating all that the reader needs to know in order to understand your perspective on the problem and your research response to it, including your reasons for researching the problem in the way in which you did (here you may need to include professional, commercial and/or ethical considerations).
- Describe the way you researched the problem (e.g. methods, materials, procedures) and give an ongoing analysis of research findings.
- Summarize the results of your research study in terms of the initial problem state and evaluate your perceptions of the problem, the way you went about tackling it, the significance of any research findings for the problem and for you as the problem solver.
- Conclude with some thoughts on any limitations/strengths of your particular research approach and any implications for further research within the general context first described.

Writer centred
- Describe how you came to the research topic (e.g. this may involve an analysis of an aspect of your professional practice).
- Analyse your experience with aspects within the topic as you researched it (perhaps taking experiential themes to maintain coherence).
- Give your reader some insight and understanding relating to your experience of researching the topic.
- Conclude with implications for you (and perhaps for your professional practice) and for future research (by you or by others).

Some conventions in academic writing about research

Writing in the third person

In academic writing about research it is usually taken to be important to be as objective as possible in dealing with issues. One way in which you can do this is to adopt a style of writing in which you avoid writing in the first person (e.g. 'I was involved in discussion . . .') and instead write in the third person (e.g. 'The author was involved . . .') or use other forms of words which avoid the use of 'I' (e.g. 'Discussions took place in which . . .'). Such styles are generally accepted within many quarters of the academic community as enabling you to distance yourself from your subject and create a feeling of objectivity. Certainly, as a general rule it is wise to avoid overuse of the first person in any academic writing. Nevertheless, in some research spheres, reflection on your own responses to situations is required and avoidance of the first person at any cost can lead to clumsy phrasing and in turn to unintelligible text. Indeed, in some areas – particularly within the qualitative research domain – the use of the first person is seen as a way of strengthening the writing and is advocated; the argument here is that the writer's voice needs to come through his or her writing. If you are the subject of your own research, with your own subjectivity as the focus of your analyses then *not* to use the first person might well mislead your readers and possibly misrepresent the way you have gone about researching. Common sense and sensitivity to context on your part therefore needs to prevail. You would be advised to check out usage of the first person in writing about your research with tutors and/or against any discipline specific guidelines on style and format.

Task: writing in the third person

- Write down a short paragraph relating, from your own personal perspective, an incident in your recent professional experience with a brief comment on how you felt about it.

- Rewrite the paragraph without using 'I', 'me' or 'my'.

Switching tense

The way in which you make use of tense can be a critical factor in whether or not your reader is able to understand readily what you are trying to say about your research. A common problem in writing clearly, especially when dealing with the reporting of complex developments over a lengthy period of research, is that of controlling the reporting of what happened during your research in such a way as to maintain appropriateness of tense. Indeed, when writing about the work of others and the status of knowledge it is necessary to hold to a system. You should use the past tense when considering the conclusions of others, e.g. 'Jones (1993) *showed* that . . .', but when writing about concepts that are established (i.e. where there is at least no significant present controversy) and have been published in the past you should use the present tense, e.g. 'Autism *is* a pervasive developmental disorder.' Varying the tense varies the status you give to particular sources and particular kinds of knowledge.

It is argued by some that writing about research should invariably be in the past tense and that the present tense should be reserved for specific directions to the reader concerning the current text (e.g. 'Here it is suggested that all children with autism are likely to . . .') and any general conclusions that can be accepted as established for whatever reason (e.g. 'It is clear that . . .'). However, you may find it more comfortable to write in the present tense and again, in some research disciplines, the kind of reflective practice that is required may involve use of the present tense at least in the introduction and the discussion sections.

One thing that is clear is that you should try to establish a use of tense which is reasonable within the context of your own research and that you then stick to throughout a piece of writing. It can be very disconcerting for the reader when tense changes without any apparent rhyme or reason – and as well as disconcerting it can be misleading. For example, when reporting on the kind of research project that analyses the development of your own ideas that arose from specific research findings you need to be accurate in your use of tense to distinguish what you believed at one point in time, from what you began to understand through the process of researching, from what you have come to believe now and indeed from what you will seek to test out in the future.

Stereotypes and derogatory terms

If you use a stereotype in your writing about research then you are in danger of conveying a misleading message or at least a message that confounds rather than clarifies an issue. For example if you write, 'A nurse has a duty to care for her patients . . .' then you are potentially misleading your reader because not all nurses are female. One way out of this is for you to use a form which includes, in this case, both genders, e.g. 'A nurse has a duty to care for his or her patients . . .'. Of course, while this is useful in some instances it can easily become cumbersome and intrusive for both you as a writer and later for your reader (e.g. 'A nurse has a duty to care for his or her patients even when he or she is burdened by a personal loss of, for example, his or her wife/husband/ partner that has left him or her emotionally distressed'). Alternatives are to adopt the plural form, e.g. 'Nurses have a duty to care for their patients . . .', or to drop the offending gender-specific pronoun, e.g. 'A nurse has a duty to care for patients . . .'.

Of course stereotyping is more pervasive and often more subtle than simply the use of pronouns. The use of 'man' rather than 'human', 'backward children' rather than 'children with learning difficulties' and 'mothering' rather than 'nurturing' are examples of terms that can be misused. It is also worth noting here that the whole issue of stereotyping and use of terms which categorize in a derogatory way is culture specific; what may be acceptable and readily understood in one cultural context may not be in another and may, in any case, change over time. This is important for you to note because the research world has been internationalized at a rapid rate over recent years as a result of the improvements in electronic communications and this means that the outcomes of your research may be expected to impact worldwide; in this sense the eventual readers of your work may be drawn from very different cultures and subcultures. Of course, you cannot be expected to accommodate every nuance of cultural meaning but I suggest that you have a duty to conform to global conventions where they exist and to write in as clear and objective way as is possible. As a writer about research you need to focus upon the need for clarity and accuracy of description. If you use a term in a way which has unseen implications for the way in which it can be interpreted by your reader, then you risk misinterpretation or misunderstanding – clarity is all.

Suggestion for further reading

Miller and Swift (1989) deal with the specific issue of non-sexist writing in some depth (see Section 3 of Further Reading).

Using jargon and specialized research terminology

There is a sense in which one researcher's jargon is another's everyday working vocabulary. Certainly, your research discipline or profession may be in some ways defined to outsiders by the breadth and scope of the specific language used (perhaps exclusively) by its practitioners. As someone who is returning to study, you have to come to terms with the way in which specialized language is used within your life outside of academia and the relationship between this and the demands of such academia. It is perfectly acceptable, indeed it may be necessary, to use, for example, technical terminology in the writing of research reports. Depending on the intended readership you may or may not have to use a device such as a glossary to explain the terms that you need to use, but there are likely to be at least some terms which will be used commonly in your particular discipline and which you can therefore use with impunity within a research programme located firmly within that discipline. However, increasingly research projects are overlapping different disciplinary or professional fields and therefore you need to be aware of the currency and limitations of particular kinds of terminology and alive to the possibilities of misunderstanding or plain bafflement on the part of your readership. Again, your purpose is to be understood, not to seem esoteric or aloof or so specialized as to be not understood by those in related areas with shared research interests.

What is not acceptable, in any discipline, is the use of convoluted sentence structures and obscure and sometimes newly created words and combinations of words to get across a message when simple structures and straightforward words can do the job just as well; that is without any loss of the fine distinctions of meaning etc.

Task: using specialized terminology

- Write a few sentences which include as many examples of what some might term your research discipline or professional jargon as you can manage (accepting that you may wish to define the words as 'specialized terminology' yourself).
- Rewrite those sentences using non-technical, non-specialized language.

Abbreviations and acronyms

Abbreviations and acronyms are widely used in society in general and, similarly, within your own discipline forms of shortening text may be prevalent, though here meaning may be restricted to those within that discipline rather than universally understood. Whatever the case, for our purposes here it seems helpful to accept that the use of abbreviations and acronyms in academic writing about research takes on an importance beyond any predilections you may have for their general use in that they may either enlighten or obscure your text according to the way in which you have used them.

Abbreviations and acronyms can be useful where, in your writing about your research, you need to make continual reference to something that has a long or complex name and which is readily abbreviated into an easily recognizable form. Obviously some abbreviations (of professional bodies for example) are commonly used and may seem therefore not to need explanation. Nevertheless you should not assume too much in this respect; for one thing terminology changes over time and also there can be confusing similarities (e.g. in the world of special schooling 'SLD' has been used to refer to 'severe learning difficulties' and also by some to 'specific learning difficulties', two terms with very different meanings). Therefore, I think that it is wise to spell out words in their entirety and give the abbreviation in parentheses at the first time of use in any writing about research. You could also make use of a glossary. Both techniques allow you to use the abbreviation alone thereafter with impunity.

It may be that you decide to generate your own form of abbreviation for something that is not commonly recognizable (particular groups of subjects in an experimental investigation for example). Again, this is allowable but the text should remain understandable; if the use of abbreviations makes it harder for your reader to follow what is going on then it is counterproductive. Similarly with acronyms: they have the advantage of being more readily remembered than some kinds of abbreviation in that they should relate to something meaningful, but over-elaborate and contrived acronyms in research write-ups can be distracting and, in my experience, ultimately irritating. In some instances (for example in case studies) pseudonyms used to describe participants can be more easily digested and retained by the reader than either abbreviations or acronyms.

Writing about research within a professional context

If you are registered for a research degree that is referenced within one of the professions, such as a professional doctorate, then there are likely to be underpinning implications that your own professional practice will be improved as a result of your programme of research study. Your writing about your research therefore will need to reflect the way in which such an improvement has been effected. My experience suggests that research degree examiners tend to look for evidence that conducting investigations and active reflection on practice has changed the relationship with a candidate's professional context in a positive sense. This is not to say that direct evidence of being better at your job will be required of you in the writing you do about your professionally based research but that your understanding of your own professional activities and the way in which they relate to other connected aspects of research has broadened and deepened and that the range of your professional skills has been extended. Further, an increased flexibility in your approach to problems within your profession that is informed by your new understanding of research methods and their implementation is typically seen as a desired outcome of engaging in professionally oriented research programmes of study. In short, I think that you would do well to try and show in your written work how your critical awareness has increased as a result of engaging in your particular programme of research study (for example that your awareness of new techniques in sampling might improve your performance as an environmental scientist or how an increased understanding of how to generate evidence in the context of modern equal opportunities legislation might improve your abilities as a personnel manager).

Using your reading

Referring and quoting

In order to acknowledge the work of other researchers in your text it is usual to either refer to their work or to quote their actual words. There is an important distinction between the use of reference and quotation, and again the relative value of their usage is open to some personal interpretation. For my part the distinction revolves around purpose.

References

Referring to other researchers in your text (see later sections for ways of doing this) is to acknowledge their work, e.g. 'Jones and Evans (1998) described their findings in terms of . . .' or 'integration in this case worked only with the involvement of peers as well as the support of staff (Nind and Powell, 1997)'. In these cases you are putting into your own words what other people have found from their research or have written about their research. If you fail to refer in this way then you run the risk of being accused of plagiarism (see separate section later in this chapter). The other reason that you need to reference is that it enables your readers to pursue ideas about research, or information on the research findings of others, for themselves in the texts that you indicate. They may wish to do this solely for their own interest, or to check that you have interpreted the referenced researcher accurately, or to check that you have not simply copied out words from the referenced text; whatever their motivation they must have the opportunity to trace your sources.

Quotations

In contrast to the notion of a reference, the purpose of a quotation is to set out the exact words used by another author because those words sum up a point or a piece of research information succinctly. In my view when you use a quote you are saying effectively that the words taken and reproduced in your work are of particular significance to your argument and cannot be reduced or improved upon by you. Further, I suggest that you would be advised to avoid the overuse of quotations when writing about your research because they can disrupt the flow of your own text and irritate your reader, who wants to know what you think and how you have interpreted the views and research findings of others rather than to read how accurately you can copy.

Some typical questions and some suggested solutions relating to the use of quotations are given in Table 8.3 on 'Questions and solutions: using quotations'.

Plagiarism

If you use material from a source in another researcher's work without acknowledgement then you are guilty of plagiarism. There is a thin but clear line between what has been described above as the proper and advantageous use of other people's research work and findings and a form of academic cheating. To stay on the right side of that line you need to be scrupulous in acknowledging your sources. It is commonplace in research degree regulations to find

Table 8.3 Questions and solutions: using quotations

Possible question	Possible solution
'How much detail do I have to give at the end of the quote that I have inserted into my text?'	You need to give the author's surname, the date and the page number(s): 'which illustrates the fluidity of the process' (Kenyon 1997: 14)
'Should I start each quote on a new line?'	Yes, and further you should, where possible, indent the quote to demarcate it from the rest of the text.
'I find I do not need to quote the whole section from the author – the important bits are at the beginning and end of the paragraph – can I cut the quote down?'	Yes, as long as you do not distort the meaning of the original; the typical device is to use an ellipsis (three dots) to indicate a cut: 'In the cross-cultural comparison made in this study it is clear that religious belief was the significant factor . . . the significance was apparent to participants themselves'.
'I want to emphasize one bit of the quote for my own purposes: can I do this and if so how?'	If it is necessary for your use of the quote, then it is possible for you to give an emphasis by italicizing or underlining the key word(s), e.g.: 'the movement was driven by industrial relations *difficulties* rather than by . . .'; you do need to add in parentheses after this kind of emphasizing a note which informs the reader that the emphasis given is yours and not the original author's: ('emphasis in original' or 'my emphasis'). This is necessary because clearly you are adding to the original text in such a way as to possibly affect the original author's intended emphasis and possibly even his or her meaning.

clauses that require examiners to challenge candidates who plagiarize in their written research submissions. In many institutions plagiarism means automatic failure.

Suggestions for further reading

For further thoughts on the way in which your reading should influence your writing, see Northedge (1990) and Raaheim et al. (1991); both are listed in Section 8 of Further Reading.

Referencing

Setting out a reference list

Of the various ways to reference work in your text the two most common are the numbering system and the author-date (sometimes referred to as the Harvard system). My experience with both methods has led me to the view that the latter is the simplest for the reader to use but again, approaches to referencing differ across disciplines and institutions and you must seek out guidelines within your own institution or department or from your supervisory team.

Numbering system

In this system you put a superscript number in the text at the point to which you wish to refer (e.g. 'the production of metals, aircraft building and armourments.[46']). Then at the end of your piece of work you list the numbers and following each you give the details of the referenced author in the same way suggested below in the section on the 'author-date system'. In this way the numbers direct your reader to the appropriate part of the references or bibliography (e.g. '46. R.F. Merton, 1963. *Social Theory* . . .'). This procedure may seem simple and it does mean that you do not clutter your text with names and dates, but it has the disadvantage for your readers that they have to keep referring to a list at the end of your submitted work in order to know which authors are being referenced. Because I have come to think of the numbering system as the less attractive of the two methods, I have decided to use the author-date system described below to explore the remaining aspects of referencing.

Author-date system

In this system you give the name of the author and the year of publication in the text; this enables your reader to refer to the list at the end of the piece of work where the reference can be found in its place within the alphabetical order, thus: 'the development of these techniques by Singh (1998) changed the way in which', or 'techniques were developed (Singh 1998) which changed the way in which'. Of course there are often subtle differences to this basic format and these are noted in Table 8.4 'Questions and solutions: referencing'.

References in an author-date system should be listed at the end of your written text (i.e. before any appendices) in alphabetical order of authors' surnames. The only thing that might come between the last part of your written text and the references might be a short acknowledgement (to individuals or institutions who have been instrumental in facilitating your research) if such is needed for a specific reason or common courtesy demands it.

Table 8.4 Questions and solutions: referencing

Possible question	Possible solution
'What happens if I want to refer to more than one article written by the same researcher in the same year?'	In your text refer to e.g. Mackay 1996a and later Mackay 1996b (and so on if necessary); then in your reference list simply list the references in the a, b, c order, including the a, b etc. after the date as in the text.
'I find that I want to refer to the same source repeatedly in a short space, do I really need to keep repeating the date every time (it seems cumbersome)?'	In some circumstances you may get away with omitting the date in an oft repeated reference within a short space in your work: 'Wong (1998) refers to a particular form of intervention and goes on to describe some of the outcomes in terms of . . . Wong also makes claims regarding . . .'. But if you are often repeating then you may need to reconsider whether or not you are being too dependent on one author; alternatively you may need to look at your style and try to make more use of (following the above example) 'she also makes claims regarding . . .' or 'in this work claims are made regarding'. An alternative is to use 'ibid.' as explained below.
'Similarly to the above I find that I am referring again to a researcher's work to which I have *just* referred, should I continue to write Stanislav (1994) even though it is beginning to sound cumbersome?'	In these circumstances you can use ibid. (an abbreviation of ibidem – 'in the same place'). It may be used *only* where it comes straight away after the work has first been identified, e.g. 'Stanislav (1994) discusses the development of new malarial drugs . . . findings about the side-effects of the drugs give cause for some concern (ibid. p. 217)'.
'In the front of the book that I want to reference there is more than one date, which one do I use?'	You need to note the date of the edition of the book to which you have referred (not the print-run date or the original publication date).
'I have read more than one author who has written about this particular aspect: should I list them all and if so how do I do that?'	If you are saying that a number of researchers have investigated a particular problem or perhaps have reached similar conclusions then you can list them together (usually in alphabetical but perhaps in chronological order if that suits your particular purpose, i.e. if chronology is significant): 'a number of authors have reported similar findings in this respect (Evans 1986; Sokhi 1994; Wheeler 1990)'.

(Continued overleaf)

Table 8.4 Continued

Possible question	Possible solution
'There are two authors of the article I wish to reference, do I note only the first author or give both names?'	If there are two authors then you need to mention both in your text: 'Tadgerouni and Whitty (1997) suggested that . . .' or again 'It has been suggested (Tadgerouni and Whitty 1997) that . . .'
'There are more than two authors of the research article that I wish to reference, how do I deal with that?'	If there are more than two authors then you need to use et al. (an abbreviated form of et alia, which means 'and others') in your text: 'Lecourt et al. (1986) describe the way in which . . .'. If there are not too many authors then you might wish to list all of them the first time you note them in the text: ('Lecourt, Maggerote and Peeters (1986) describe . . .') and then use et al. for any further references. However, even if you use et al. in the text, you must list all the authors (however many there are) in the reference list at the end of your work.
'Do I use first names as well as surnames when referring to authors?'	No: if you suddenly use a first name rather than the surname only, then you are proffering some special, but undefined, status on the particular researcher. However, if two individual authors have the same surname, use their initials (B. Jones 1986; M. Jones 2001).

The reference list

You will not be surprised to hear that there are many variations on the way in which author-date references are set out. A fairly standard method is offered in Table 8.5 on 'Setting out references'. However, I should stress that your institution or department may subscribe to a specific system and there may be regulations dictating the way in which you must employ full stops, commas, colons, semi-colons, parentheses, italicized print and the positioning of the date in ways which differ from the method given in Table 8.5. The important thing is to follow any system that is laid down in your institution (and follow it from the start of your research programme) and where one is not defined in regulations then to follow what is commonly accepted within your discipline or is advised by your supervisor. At all times you should aim for consistency and clarity.

Table 8.5 Setting out references

Kind of source being referenced	Example of a format
Single-authored book	Donaldson, M. (1978) *Children's Minds*. London: Fontana. (Note: italics should be used rather than underlining for book titles)
Edited book	Zuckerman, H., Cole, J.R. and Bruer, J.T. (eds) (1991) *The Outer Circle*. New York: W.W. Norton.
Chapter in an edited book	Blackman, D.E. (1984) The current status of behaviourism and learning theory in psychology, in D. Fontana (ed.) *Behaviourism and Learning Theory in Education*, pp. 3–14. Edinburgh: Scottish Academic Press. (Note: you need to use italics to indicate the book where the chapter can be found)
Single-authored article in a journal	Wing, L. (1981) Asperger's Syndrome: a clinical account. *Journal of Psychological Medicine, 11*: 115–129. (Note: you need to use italics to indicate the journal where the article can be found)
Multi-authored article	Atkinson, P.A., Reid, M.E. and Sheldrake, P.F. (1977) Medical mystique. *Sociology of Work and Occupations, 4* (3): 307–322.

Suggestions for further reading

By way of supplementary reading of the issues raised in this chapter, I draw your attention to Sections 3 and 8 of Further Reading, in particular Canter and Fairbairn (2006) in Section 3 and Murray (2004, 2006) in Section 8, all of which contain information about how to enhance your abilities as a writer about research.

Summary

- You have considered the planning of written work as an integral part of the whole process of study.
- You have worked through some aspects of the preparatory stages to writing, including difficulties in getting started.
- You have considered the usefulness of some of the conventions of academic writing.
- You have made links between academic writing and professional development.

- You have considered details of the techniques for effective quoting and referencing.
- You have thought about how to prepare written work for submission by minimizing your errors and maximizing your accessibility as a writer.

Conclusion

If you are to make clear to your reader what it is that you want to convey about your research then you must first be clear about that message yourself. In this chapter I have dealt with 'effective writing' but such a notion would be somewhat hollow without a clear understanding on your part as to intended meanings and, of course, without some merit in terms of content.

I have dealt with the process of academic writing about research and have tried to show ways in which you can make your own writing about your research more effective. Laurence Sterne in *Tristram Shandy* conceptualized writing as 'conversation' and my suggestion to you is that you would do well to treat those who read about your research with the same kind of consideration that you would offer to conversational partners – by taking into account what those partners already know and what they need to know in order to understand what it is that you wish to say.

9

Constructing and presenting your research in a written submission

Overview • Introduction • Establishing a thesis • What does academic researching entail? • Constraints on a final research degree submission • Writing a dissertation title • Writing an abstract • Using graphics • Academic investigation and professional progress • Summary • Conclusion

> *An intellectual is someone whose mind watches itself.*
> Albert Camus (1913–1960), *Carnets* (1935–1942)

Overview

All research degrees at UK universities include the need to produce a major piece of research-based work (and here those working within towards a professional doctorate are not excluded, though parameters may vary). This chapter deals with this particular stage of any research degree programme. In this chapter, therefore, you will be asked to:

- consider the purpose behind the writing of a research dissertation and the kinds of demand it is likely to make upon you (including personally and professionally)
- think through (where applicable) the relationship between your research programme (which results in a written dissertation) and the development of your own professional practice
- consider, in particular, the title and the abstract of your submitted research work.

Introduction

Your programme of research study will culminate, invariably, in a substantial piece of work in which you will be expected to show how much you have learned about research during the whole of your period of study at the university. This is a defining feature of a 'research degree' as opposed to a 'taught' mode of study. The only variation will be in how significant this submission is within the overall assessment. For the majority of research degree programmes the 'final submission' and its defence will carry all of the weight of assessment and whatever interim assessments may have taken place (e.g. progression, transfer and upgrade phases) they will have no direct bearing on your chances of success or failure. In order to stress here the singular importance of the final submission I note that in most institutions examiners are not informed of any progress issues; in short they mark blind of whatever has occurred in these terms since initial registration and are concerned only with the final piece of work. However, in many of the professional doctorates this situation will not be so clear-cut and the final submission may be seen as part of the entirety of assessment spaced over the whole of the registered period of study; you may need to have passed successfully any number of other, sometimes related, assignments or minor research projects. Similarly, some research masters programmes may involve an accumulation of pieces of research work towards a final view of the candidate as successful or not in meeting the criteria for the award.

Because of the variations noted above, you may find that the final piece of work is described as an extended case study, major project, portfolio, research report, dissertation or thesis. To confuse the issue a portfolio would normally contain a number of pieces of work, one of which might be considerably more substantial than the rest (and carry the name of one of the other items in the list above). Institutions differ in the way that they employ the various terms noted above. In the case of this particular terminology, Alice (in Wonderland) was correct in noting that words 'can mean what you want them to mean'. However, it is also the case that here definitions do matter and you need to read what your institutional regulations say about what is required of a research degree submission at the level (e.g. masters or doctoral) and the kind (e.g. professional doctorate or PhD) which you intend to submit.

Suggestions for further reading

You might wish to supplement your reading of this chapter with a reference to publications cited in Sections 3 and 8 of Further Reading, particularly Murray (2006) in Section 3 and Hampson (1994) in Section 8.

Establishing a thesis

The notion of thesis

A thesis is an intellectual position that you choose to hold. However, the word is also commonly used across the sector to mean the bound submission that you hand in for assessment. In my view (which may well be idiosyncratic on this point) this latter is an unfortunate use of the term because it obscures the purposes of research study and the assessment of it. You will engage in research and as part of that process you will develop an intellectual position (thesis) that you will be prepared, eventually, to defend. I should note here that, while you may think that you have your position established at the outset of your studies, this flies in the face of real research enterprise where ideas are developed through investigation not merely confirmed by it. Your research then enables you to develop an argument that supports your position. That argument may comprise evidence that arises from investigation.

What you submit for assessment is, therefore, not only a statement of your chosen intellectual position (your thesis), but also the argument that supports it (the evidence supplied by your research). As a candidate for a research degree you are expected to 'hold forth' on both, that is, on both your position and your argument. In the formal sense you dissertate on the combination of both and hence the word 'dissertation' is often used to describe the entirety of what is submitted for assessment. In this book I use the terms 'the submission' and 'dissertation' interchangeably to indicate what is submitted.

The important point to make here is that it is in the intellectual position you take that the originality of your work should be evident.

Task: stating your thesis

Write down in a few sentences the intellectual position that you think you will take in your final submission (note that this will be in the form of a proposition rather than a question, i.e. 'My position is that . . .').

Developing an argument to support your thesis

The argument that you develop to support your thesis should be based on a rational exploration of all the pertinent issues. It is not therefore merely a matter of setting down what you did in your research (describing a series of experiments for example), rather you are required to assemble your workings into a coherent argument that deals with evidence in a fair and even-handed way and which takes account of what others working in the field have found (however inconvenient their findings might be for your thesis).

Your dissertation needs to be set out in such a way as to clearly signpost to your readers what your thesis is and how it is supported by your argument. Indeed, if you are given the opportunity to present an oral overview of your dissertation at the outset of your viva then you need to take that opportunity to state your thesis and spell out the main thread of your argument(s).

Task: the argument in support of your thesis

In a simple bullet point list, note down the arguments that you intend to make in support of the intellectual position that you have identified (in the previous task).

Defending your thesis

The final part of the defence of your thesis takes place at your oral examination. This is dealt with in some detail in Chapter 10 but suffice to say here that, in that examination, you have the opportunity to state your case and argue for it. In the UK system it is the function of your examiners to question both your position and your argument. There is a sense in which 'defence' is an unfortunate word to use here because it may imply that you should be defensive; in fact it is better to conceive of this event as a discussion of your thesis and its supporting argument, albeit a discussion set in an adversarial mode.

The whole point is that research is about the generation of ideas based on evidence and studying about research through doing it is, therefore, a matter of learning not only how to, for example, gather and analyse data but also how to establish what the data mean and finally how to defend your interpretation of that meaning.

What does academic researching entail?

Suggestions for further reading
To supplement your reading of this section you might like to refer to texts noted in Further Reading where issues of clear thinking and a systematic approach are discussed. In general terms, Potter (2006) (see Section 1) offers excellent advice; for those working in the social sciences Phelan and Reynolds (1995) (see Section 9) is a useful text.

Self-critical awareness

Research degree level work typically implies that there will be a dimension present within the way in which you submit your work for assessment in which you exhibit self-awareness about how your research study was conceived and carried out and the implications arising from the kinds of choices you made in defining and pursuing your research questions. Your submission therefore needs to reflect this. Mistakes and disappointing levels of result are less significant when you achieve high levels of critical analysis of the processes and procedures that you instigated and pursued in your studies. My contention is that you need to make overt in your write-up the kind of process Albert Camus (see quotation at the start of the chapter) was alluding to when he wrote of 'the mind watching itself'. Camus was referring to what it means to be an intellectual rather than specifically a researcher; nevertheless, I think it is legitimate to take his words to refer here to the researcher specifically because researching is after all, just one process of intellectualizing. As a researcher it seems to me that your mind needs to 'watch itself', as Camus suggests, and, in turn, your submission needs to make apparent that ongoing process of reflection.

It may help here to note that there are often two levels operating when examiners consider a piece of research degree work: on the one hand they want to know what has been found out and how significant that is and on the other they want to know how much you, as a research student, have learnt through the process of researching. This is why I suggest that you pay particular attention to explaining clearly why you did what you did and why you think that you found what you found and how undertaking all of the research work has affected your own understanding of the problem itself, the methodologies employed and your own ways of working within your research discipline.

Empirical and philosophical investigations

There may seem to you to be an underlying assumption in some of what I have written in this chapter that the dissertation has involved some investigation 'in the field' resulting in empirical data (i.e. data that relate to information gained through experience rather than from abstract reflection). It may be of course that your research dissertation might investigate, or perhaps more properly 'interrogate', theoretical standpoints on a specific topic in the extant literature. In this latter sense the way in which you write up your research processes and findings in a dissertation will need to add to how your reader (which is, primarily if not entirely, your examiner) is able to understand that topic at an intellectual level that is not necessarily dependent on the collection and analysis of data. It would, however, be misleading of me to distinguish too rigidly between empirical and philosophical investigation. If you engage in empirical data-gathering then it is likely to be founded on conceptual understandings that may have been clarified at a philosophical level just as any philosophical investigation you undertake might be based on an argument about how to clarify empirically based understandings. The point I am making here is that while empirical inquiry requires data relating to questions or hypotheses, philosophical inquiry requires critical argument or debate: both require investigation and both may properly be described as 'research'.

Constraints on a final research degree submission

There is little doubt that when you come to decide on the form of your final submission and on the kinds of research that will underpin it, you would be advised to consider carefully what you will not be able to do as well as what you will. Of course there are always constraints on any piece of academic work and indeed, the key problem of working within a predetermined word length was noted in an earlier chapter, but a dissertation can pose particular problems in this respect because it may be the first time in your academic life that you have been asked to make decisions for yourself about the kind of topic to be investigated and the remit of that topic.

Time and resources

It is important that you make realistic decisions about the time and the resources that you have available to be dedicated to the research that you are designing. In particular, you need to consider any limits on the duration of your research programme. If your proposed research study involves some action on your part (and especially action that is an intervention in an aspect of the normal professional process) then you will need to recognize that measured action takes time to devise, test, pilot, put into effect and importantly may need to take place consistently over a substantial period of time if any effects are to be identifiable or measurable.

Ethical boundaries

The kind of study that you engage in at dissertation level is likely to have an investigative component and there may be ethical implications; you therefore need to consider the parameters of the study in terms of any ethical considerations and this I have already touched upon in Chapter 6. These considerations might range from the ethics of business management, to relationships with clients, to privileged knowledge, to environmental 'green' issues, to animal rights. In the presenting of your research for assessment you need to incorporate the way in which you approached the ethical dimension to your work, the measures you took to ensure that the work avoided anything that might be unethical and any impacts on the design of your research that arose because of ethical concerns. In making a judgement about how much you have learnt about doing research the examiners will want to know how much you have learnt about the need to remain within ethical boundaries and how that impacts on research possibilities in your future work and indeed that of others in your field. 'Ethics' are not minor matters that can be dealt with in 'getting approval' and then quietly forgotten. They are an integral part of doing research and as such need to be an integral part of the presentation of your research work. I have known research students fail to include any mention of the ethical dimension to their work in their final submission on the grounds that 'permission was granted'. Frankly, this is not good enough.

In Table 9.1 on 'Ethical issues: human participants' I give some examples of the kinds of generic issues in relation to the ethics of doing research work that involves human participants because these are likely to have widest applicability. Please note that this list is not intended to be in any way inclusive. I am merely giving examples of the kinds of issues that may arise and that would need to be addressed in any final submission.

Task: ethical issues
- List any ethical issues that are likely to arise in your research studies (or have arisen).
- Beside each issue listed, note down how you will address it (or how you have addressed it).

Need to generalize findings

A key issue to be considered at the planning stage of the dissertation is whether or not there is a need for your findings to be generalizable. If you need to show not only that something happens under a set of circumstances but also that the same thing is likely to happen under other similar but different circumstances, then your task takes on a new dimension which requires that you pay particular attention to the way in which you set up your study and the way in

Table 9.1 Ethical issues: human participants

These are some of the issues you may need to include in the writing up of any project involving human subjects:
- The basic need to ensure that no harm of any kind came to people as a result of their participation in your investigation.
- The consent of those subjects to taking part, which needed to have been given with an ever present option of withdrawal (this can be a particularly sensitive issue if you had been dealing with people who may have difficulty in giving informed consent, e.g. individuals with learning difficulties).
- Difficulties that arose whenever there was any deliberate deception in your investigation – for example where you intend not to tell subjects why you are asking your questions (I should note here that many would consider any such deliberate deception unethical).
- How you were able to debrief your subjects and deal with any difficulties that arose in the process of that debriefing.
- Maintaining the confidentiality of any information given to you by subjects, respecting the privacy of any participants in your investigation and generally protecting them from any harm that might have arisen from your questioning or from your results (this can be a particularly sensitive issue if you had been asking people in the workplace about, for example, management techniques or production qualities).
- How you resolved any tensions between your professional duty to advise any member of a client group as the need to do so became apparent and any requirement in your investigation to remain aloof from a situation that you were observing (or indeed what you did if you discovered that a participant needs, and is entitled to, a particular form of help that they are not getting – yet you feel that it is not your place as an outside investigator to tell them or anyone else).

which you report it. For example you will need to consider the sample or the situation that you investigate to ensure that it is representative of the whole, e.g. is the group of pregnant women you have interviewed about diet representative of all women everywhere? The finer points of a requirement for generalizability need pursuing in the context of your disciplinary area, I hope it is sufficient here to note that *if* generalizability is required of your dissertation then you will be constrained in terms of the question(s) you pursue as well as the sample you investigate, your method of gathering data and the way in which you analyse and later present your results. Please note that I am not suggesting that generalizability of findings *is* always necessary or even desirable: the study of pregnant women could be valid even if your sample included a high proportion from a defined ethnic subgroup, or a particular age group or a particular geographic area which has its own dietary customs. What is important is that you recognize the nature of your sample for what it is and only make claims that address that nature.

When you write up your research you need to pay particular attention to the way in which you use words so as to stay within the bounds of what you have shown from your research rather than what you might like to have shown. Sometimes it may be reasonable to speculate or hypothesize, but when you do this you need to make clear to your reader that this is precisely what you are doing and why. If you conflate evidenced findings with speculative comment you run the risk of undermining the integrity of both; the reader is likely to be confused and may draw the conclusion that you cannot distinguish between kinds of evidence and the boundaries of reasonable hypothesis based on evidence.

Need to isolate factors

Another constraining dimension is the degree to which your study is required to isolate factors within the setting under investigation. It may be that central to your research question is the need to focus on one aspect of a complex situation and to separate it out from other factors or interactions (for example to isolate the genetic component in the development of a physical condition that is also affected by environmental factors or to isolate the role a particular breed of fish plays in a developing ecosystem). To do this requires a particular kind of design in which controlling the variables and eliminating, as far as possible, confounding factors becomes paramount. This is in contrast to the kind of study where it is precisely the interaction of all the factors in the given context that is of interest (for example a study of bereavement in a particular culture in which changing attitudes to death as a result of cross-cultural influences conflicts with accepted practices and rituals). In this latter case to separate out one feature for examination in isolation of the other factors would be self-defeating.

Again, when you write up your research within the context of an academic research degree award you must spell out in sufficient detail your response to the issue of the isolation of factors. It cannot be assumed that you understand where your research sits in terms of the breadth of possibilities in this respect. You need to be explicit and you need to show that you understand the implications of your stance in this respect for the conclusions you can draw legitimately from your 'findings'. It is not, therefore, so much that one way is 'wrong' and the other 'right' (although in some disciplines common practice may well lie consistently in one direction) but rather that particular research questions require particular methodological approaches if they are to answered satisfactorily and, importantly for us here, the way that you write up your research needs to indicate not only that your research reflected a reasonable approach to the chosen research question but also that you understand the processes that make that approach reasonable and consequently would have made another approach unreasonable.

Academic insularity

It is perfectly reasonable for there to be a departmental research ethos and indeed you may have been attracted to your academic institution because it promulgates a particular set of beliefs and ways of conducting research with which you tend to concur. But there is an ever present danger of a shared view (of the kinds of research question that are worth asking as well as of the kinds of research methodologies used to answer them) becoming the dominant and then the exclusive view. If this happens then I suggest that the resulting ideological narrowness can be a problem for you as a research student. You have returned to study, in part at least, to broaden your mind and actively to take on different perspectives rather than simply absorb a set of accepted wisdoms. In the sense that your research degree should be a training in how to be a researcher then it needs to show you the breadth of possibilities and the strengths and weaknesses of varying methodological approaches. Indeed, my use of the term 'show you' may be inadequate here; your programme of research training needs to give you opportunities to test out for yourself such possibilities and come to understand them thoroughly through that testing. In matters of research methodology, awareness is not enough; you need to become familiar, to the point of mastery, with the various forms of approach and subsequent argument. Again, all of this needs to be evident in your written submission; your examiners need to be convinced that you understand both what you have done in your research and what you can, legitimately, claim from it.

If you are to avoid your dissertation being confined by any particular set of ideological beliefs about research then I suggest that it will help if you can read opposing views on issues and on the appropriateness of differing methodologies. Examiners may be drawn from the breadth of academic belief systems and prejudices and will not necessarily concur with any departmental ethos that exists in your institution. You need to be able to argue and justify the position(s) that you took in your research; you cannot rely on your examiners sharing any narrow ideological preferences that are prevalent in your department. This is, of course, another strong argument for you to take your research out of the confines of your institution and discuss it in wider fora; giving papers at external conferences is an example of this and I hope you can see from the above the value of such external exposure of your ideas and findings.

Task: operating within a dominant ideology

- Can you identify any predominant methodology or intellectual stance within which your research studies are framed?
- If you can identify in this way, then is this in any way problematic and if it is then what can you do in your submission to alleviate the problem?

Addressing word limits

In the various kinds of writing about your research that you engage in as a research student you will find yourself needing to write within word limits. This applies to most refereed journals to which you might submit research papers as well as to progress reports and certainly to the final research degree submission itself. It is worth, therefore, considering some ways in which you may restrict or cut text so as to meet any limits on word length that may be set down. You can be assured of one thing: word limits do matter. You would be unwise to ignore them and assume that you might get away with writing more than is 'allowed'. Many journal referees will refuse to even read a paper that is clearly over length and most university research degree regulations will either overtly or covertly support any examiner who refuses to assess a research submission on the grounds that it is over length (or is inappropriately presented). Indeed, publishers of books such as this that you are reading will not accept submitted manuscripts that exceed the contractually agreed word length. The argument that 'my work is impossible to fit into the word length stipulated for reason x' is simply not valid. Word length restrictions will have been set down for a reason; they apply to all researchers in the specific circumstance and are part of the rigour to which you need to apply yourself. It is often easier to write a long piece than a short one. Writing within a stipulated length is an important part of learning to be a researcher and its usefulness continues beyond research degree study. It is therefore a skill that you need to master.

When considering how to keep a piece that you are writing short or shorten a draft that you have produced, there are various tactics that you might employ:

- Take out any unnecessary background information (e.g. you need to tell your readers only what they need to know of the context in order to judge the appropriateness of your research design and the efficacy of your implementation of it).
- Remove any unnecessary sections that define aspects of the subject in hand (think through carefully what you can reasonably assume that your readership already knows).
- Reduce the amount of description surrounding the main research issue (e.g. cut to the main point without going through all of the historical process by which you arrived it – assuming that process is not the crux of the research itself).
- Consider if tables, lists, diagrams etc. can be used instead of prose.
- Look closely at the introduction (experience has shown that it is here that verbosity may lurk).
- See if any whole paragraphs can be omitted without losing overall sense and without lessening the impact of the work in terms of describing and defending your research.
- Try to précis some whole paragraphs into one or two sentences.
- See if any two paragraphs can be merged and reduced by combining points into one meaningful issue.

Clearly, how you cut a first draft to fit the size required will depend on a whole range of issues relating to the purpose of the piece and the way in which you have gone about addressing the various issues, but a good general piece of advice is to step back from the writing and ask yourself 'What do I really need to say here?' and then, 'Is all of what I have written absolutely necessary to get across what I need to say?' Often research students complain of the mental anguish felt when having to cut text but experience shows that such cutting results very frequently in a recognized improvement in their work.

Suggestions for further reading

The issues considered above in relation to the construction of a final submission are discussed in various of the publications listed in Further Reading, e.g. Longman and Hall (2008), Murray (2006) and Hampson (1994) (see Sections 1, 3 and 8 respectively).

Writing a dissertation title

The title of a research degree submission is important for a number of reasons. At a pragmatic level it is the first thing that many readers encounter and it needs to attract them to read your work in a realistic way. In a similar vein, when your examiners are chosen they agree to examine, and are eventually formally appointed to examine, the work as indicated in the title. The title becomes part therefore of an informal contract. I have known instances where an examiner refused to examine a dissertation when it arrived on her desk because, in her view, the content of the submission did not conform to the expectations established by the title. This may be an extreme example but it does indicate the importance of the title in the research degree submission process. At a less extreme level, dissertation titles are often a bone of contention at the final examination stage when it is not uncommon for examiners to complain about overlong, misleading or opaque titles. Their recommendation sometimes includes a note to the effect that the existing title needs amendment. It is part of their duty to ensure that the title reflects accurately the content and argument of the submission and that therefore what is recorded at the British Library and elsewhere is appropriate to the work. It is also necessary for the title to stand the test of time; research degree submissions are referred to by other researchers indefinitely and hence a title that contains words that are current but liable to change with changing fashions are likely to be inappropriate (of course, all words are open to changes in meaning over time but some are more transient than others and such transience is to be avoided in the matter of dissertation titles). So, while it may seem that writing a title for your submission is the least of your worries, experience has shown that it is not. It has an importance that far outweighs its physical length.

A research dissertation title needs to be succinct yet convey the meaning of the work being submitted accurately and without ambiguity (unless ambiguity is deliberate and serves a clear purpose in relation to the underlying thesis). It also needs to be understandable by peers within your discipline. It should also be contrived so as to suggest the underlying thesis (intellectual position) that is being defended in the submission. It should not be so long as to be unmanageable (remembering it has to fit on the spine of the final bound submission) or unintelligible.

A useful way that my own research students have found of starting to work out their title is to set down the key words that they think indicate what their work is about and where it is to be located within the area of the discipline. If you follow this strategy then you will need to pare down this initial list until you have a list that contains *only* those that are essential for an understanding to be gained by your reader. Then it is a matter of arranging those words into a form that is grammatically correct and that conveys the message of the work appropriately. You need to avoid titles that are so short as to become opaque and equally titles that are so long as to be cumbersome.

Task: constructing a title from key words
- Note down the key words that are *necessary* for a reader to understand what your project is about.
- Can you now use only those key words to construct a title that is *sufficient* for a reader to understand what your project is about (clearly you may need to add some prepositions and even verbs so that it makes sense but you should try to avoid the addition of any further substantive words)?

Dissertation titles

This section gives some examples of poor, weak and good titles. If the topic of a dissertation is 'how the North Sea has been affected by industrial pollution', then a number of titles are possible with varying levels of appropriateness and effectiveness:

- 'How the North Sea has been affected by industrial pollution' – poor title because it sounds like a topic rather than a title (which of course it is).
- 'Industrial pollution' – poor title because the subject matter is not clearly defined.
- 'Industrial Pollution in the North Sea' – weak title because it could relate to a number of topics (e.g. how the waste came to be in the North Sea – how to get rid of it – whether or not it is there in significant amounts).
- 'Industrial pollution haunts North Sea users' – inappropriate title because it is more akin to what is required in journalism than academia; it is not related directly to the topic and includes words that might mislead (e.g. 'haunts' is not used in its proper sense and 'users' is ill defined).

- 'An investigation into the long-term and short-term effects of any leakage of Industrial Pollution into the North Sea' – a title that is much too long; the first three words are redundant (and will almost always be so in any dissertation title because it is accepted that an investigation has been involved) and the distinction between long-term and short-term effects is all encompassing and therefore meaningless.
- 'The effects of industrial pollution in the North Sea' – good title because it is understandable and summarizes the content without redundant words (though arguably you might drop the first 'the').

Writing an abstract

The use of an abstract was mentioned in Chapter 8, where I advocated the usefulness of summarizing content before the reader begins the main part of the text. At the final submission stage of a research degree an abstract is most likely to be a requirement (I know of no institution that does not require an abstract) and therefore deserves special attention here.

An abstract is a self-contained synopsis of a piece of work. It is presented at the beginning of your submission though it will usually be the last thing in the dissertation to be written. It is necessarily short, typically with a strict maximum word length specified (e.g. 150 or 200 words) or the constraint that it must fit on to one side of A4. I have used the term 'abstract' here but alternatives with much the same meaning are synopsis, summary and overview. Whatever terminology is employed within your university, the summarizing piece of text will invariably need to contain the following:

- The main activity of the study
- The scope of the work
- A minimal amount of information about the methodology where necessary to understand in broad terms what was done and why (e.g. it might be necessary to state that a particular experimental design had been used so that the reader can understand the significance and the limitations of results)
- An outline of the most important results, outcomes or findings of the study
- A summary statement of any conclusions or recommendations that can be made.

I hope that the bullet points above illustrate to you that an abstract should contain a summary of all of the main points of the dissertation but should not go into any details or qualifications or elaboration on those points. It should be designed to force home the critical issues of the research rather than analyse the content.

In the box 'Contents of an abstract' by way of example, I take an abstract from an article that happens to be on my desk at the time of writing and deconstruct it in the terms of the requirements of an abstract that I have just listed – using the same bullet points.

Contents of an abstract

The italicized words are taken from Atkinson, S. (1998) Cognitive style in the context of design and technology project work. *Educational Psychology, 18* (2), 183–194.

- The main activity of the study ('*The intention of this article is to examine three strands of research concerning the relationship between pupil cognitive style (as assessed by the Cognitive Styles Analysis) and the following factors: pupil performance in GCSE technology examination project work; teaching strategy; teacher and pupil motivation*').
- The scope of the work ('*The research was investigated with a sample of 112 15–16-year-old pupils (85 boys and 27 girls) selected from eight schools*').
- A minimal amount of information about the methodology where necessary to understand in broad terms what was done and why (this is not present in my exemplar and, in terms of the journal in which it was published, it was probably not necessary).
- An outline of the most important results, outcomes or findings of the study ('*Analysis of the data collected indicated that a pupil's cognitive style did affect their ability to perform in GCSE design and technology project work*').
- A summary statement of any conclusions or recommendations that can be made ('*The teaching strategy adopted was shown to have differing effects upon a pupil's performance depending upon the cognitive style of that pupil. The data also indicated that the relationship between a pupil's motivation and their teacher's motivation was affected by a pupil's cognitive style*').

In this case I suggest that there are no significant differences between the structure of this abstract of a research article and that of your research degree submission – except that the latter will need to encompass more research, undertaken over a longer period of time.

Using graphics

Your final submission is likely to become a very complex as well as a lengthy piece of work and because of this you may find it useful to employ graphical representation of one kind or another to simplify ideas, to describe a mass of material succinctly or to give your reader access to large amounts of data at a glance. For example, you might use the following:

- Pictographs or flowcharts to describe organizations, processes, and cause and effect relationships (e.g. the way in which energy gets distributed throughout an engineering process).
- Graphs to compare and contrast features within the context of the study, describe changes in the state of phenomena or describe the proportions of different aspects of the study (e.g. the different scores gained by subjects over a period of time covering a series of different interventions).
- Schematic illustrations to describe parts of a whole or the whole of an operational procedure (e.g. the different roles played by participants in a emergency planning scenario).

You should not eschew using graphic representations just because these are not commonplace in your discipline; the salience of the notion that 'a picture is worth a thousand words' can be modified and applied here. Your aim is to simplify and explain your work to your reader and you need to use whatever devices enable you to do this; sometimes words can be replaced by other modes of presentation with useful effects.

Task: use of graphical representation

Are graphical representations commonplace in your research discipline?

- If yes, then what do you need to do in order to control their use so as to make them most effective in getting across your message?
- If no, then is there any scope for the use of some graphical representation in your submission – to help the readers more effectively get to grips with what you are trying to convey?

Suggestions for further reading

If you are going to make use of technical or scientific data in your dissertation then I recommend that you read Sides (1992): see Section 3 of Further Reading.

Academic investigation and professional progress

This section refers specifically to those readers who have come to their research degree studies from a professional background. But again, as noted earlier in this book, I am deliberately taking a wide definition of professions. My basic premise is that the points I make below need to be made evident by those of you from the professions in your final submission at research degree level.

The proactive profession

I think I can afford to make the assumption that one of the essential elements of a profession is that it seeks self-improvement or at the very least seeks to accommodate to changes in society while retaining its integrity and its overall efficiency. In this sense any profession to which you may belong needs to be proactive rather than simply reactive to changes that occur and the kind of proaction that is required if it is to survive and prosper needs to be based on intellectual reflection and research processes (whether that research relates to evidence-based information or theory-based conceptualization). It follows from this that if innovations in procedures, materials or processes are to be successfully integrated into the armoury of your particular profession then they need to be tested out rigorously by it in realistic situations that will indicate possibilities and implications. Such testing needs to be made explicit in your submission as appropriate.

It would be unprofessional to adopt an innovation that had never been reliably tested or that had no rationale to distinguish it from other new approaches. This would not be to say however that innovations are never adopted in this way. Indeed when discussing the ideas in this book one student (a nurse) described her view of innovations:

> The reforms in nursing began in the early 1980s. They were not scientifically thought through or piloted in some areas with the consequence that they have to be amended. This is costly and damaging to patients. Resources were not provided in adequate amounts. Professionals in the area were fed up. This has deflected attention from some good aspects of change. Innovations are often politically motivated and this has not always been good.

I have made the points above about the proactive profession because I want to argue that researching within the academic context for an academic award should mirror the kind of evaluation and examination that goes on in your professional domain. Of course, in the best of all possible worlds each would feed into the other: professional development would be influenced by research findings from within academic contexts and academia in turn would be influenced by data and concepts derived from professional work in the field.

Identifying an agenda for change

I do not think it is too pious to expect that if you engage in research that relates to your professional work and results in some form of dissertation then that investigation should assist you in identifying an agenda for achieving positive change in your professional context. For example, in my view, you should be able to use the research your undertake for your academic award for the following kinds of end:

- To clarify issues that are problematic in your professional work
- To unravel the implications and knock-on effects of contrasting approaches or the introduction of new materials
- To evaluate new ideas and practices in terms of their efficacy
- To identify new directions for future, worthwhile avenues for investigation.

Another key aspect of the professional and academic research interface is the interdisciplinary dimension already discussed. Increasingly, professionals work alongside, or at least in the same arena as, colleagues from other disciplines and professions. If this is true for you then academic research study should give you the opportunity to explore the boundaries of your discipline and to consider the way in which your profession can relate to others. Where appropriate such exploration needs to form part of your research degree submission. Some of my students have reported that learning to talk to those from other areas for the purposes of conducting research that impacts at the points of contact between disciplines has involved not only contriving a shared language but also coming to understand the attitudes and driving forces behind the activities of other professional groups and other researchers.

Suggestions for further reading

If you are interested in the professional dimensions to research degree study that have been outlined here, you might wish to refer to Scott et al. (2004): see Section 7 of Further Reading.

Summary

- You have come to a clearer understanding about the purpose behind the kinds of investigation that typically comprise your programme of research study.
- You have considered the various kinds of constraint that are likely to operate on your investigations and on your writing up.

- You have given some thought to the title and the abstract of your final research degree submission.
- You have linked academic investigation with professional progress where appropriate.

Conclusion

A good research degree submission might be one in which there is evidence of a clear rationale underpinning a thorough investigation (be that of a philosophical or empirical kind) resulting in correctly interpreted results, all reported accurately and concisely. An excellent dissertation however will contain all of these things but will offer, in addition, an ongoing reflective discourse on the way in which you yourself have been affected by the process of engaging in the research and have thus developed as a researcher. Camus may not have been thinking of students returning to research degree studies when he wrote of the mind watching itself but I suggest that his maxim is useful nonetheless. Researching is a process of intellectualizing in the way that Camus identified and, in his terms, I think it is useful for you to think of yourself as someone whose mind gives careful scrutiny not only to the outcomes of your research but also to your own developing understanding of the processes of researching. In this sense a lot of what has been said in this chapter about the development of ideas, the working within constraints and so on needs to be made explicit in the way in which you write up your research and thus justify your claim for the research degree award in question.

10

Being examined at research degree level

Overview • Introduction • Distinctiveness of the research degree examination process • Typical processes and procedures of submission for assessment • Submitting your work for assessment • Assessment of your written submission and of you as a research degree candidate • Pragmatic features of the oral examination (viva) • Likely outcomes and activities subsequent to the viva • Summary • Conclusion

> *It is better to debate a question without settling it than to settle a question without debating it.*
>
> Joseph Joubert (1754–1824), *Pensées* (1888)

Overview

This chapter addresses the way in which research degrees are examined in the UK. It gives you the kind of information needed to make the experience a positive one. In this chapter, therefore, you will be asked to:

- reflect on the processes and procedures of research degree examination in the UK
- consider what is involved in the assessment of your written submission and of you as a research degree candidate

- analyse the purposes and likely features of the oral examination (viva)
- rehearse the likely outcomes and activities subsequent to the viva (e.g. possible amendments to your written submission).

Introduction

Most universities hold very dear the whole process of research degree examination and particularly of the appointment of examiners for research degrees; this latter aspect is their ultimate control over the quality of their most prestigious awards. In any study that is assessed by single, final assessment only (i.e. most research degree study) then the role of examiners becomes crucial and this is particularly so in the case of external examiners because they are there to ensure that the standards of your particular university are in line with those to be found elsewhere in the UK higher education system. In this chapter I will go into some detail as to why universities act in the way that they do in the examination of research degrees. My reasoning here is that it will help you to cope with the process effectively if you understand why it works as it does.

In this chapter I am referring to the final examination only. I am not referring to earlier examinations of one kind or another that may occur in some professional doctoral programmes (not that they lack in importance but space does not permit me to deal with them in this text).

Also, it is important for me to note before I become embroiled in trying to unravel the mechanics of research degree examination that there is a basic purpose to all of this that transcends the 'testing' of you as a candidate. It is the case that research needs to be questioned and hence you as the researcher likewise. Indeed, to leave research unquestioned would be to fall into the trap indicated by Joubert in the quotation above: that is, one would be in danger of settling a question (e.g. agreeing on your findings) without debate. Whether or not definitive answers about the substantive issues to which your research relates come out of your viva is not the point, what matters is that the questions you have sought to answer in your work are debated fully and without prejudice rather than settled without debate. You perhaps need to conceive of this assessment part of your research degree journey as an integral part of engaging in research – the questioning and debating part.

Suggestions for further reading

Your reading of this chapter would be supplemented by reference to Section 6 of Further Reading, which lists books and articles devoted to the topic of research degree examination, research findings on the topic, opinion pieces and guidance for candidates, their supervisors and for examiners.

Distinctiveness of the research degree examination process

I will not spend too long in spelling out the distinctiveness of research degree examination because many of the features that distinguish it have already been touched upon in earlier sections on the distinctiveness of this kind of study in general. Suffice it to say then that the distinctiveness identified earlier extends to the domain of the examination. To summarize (and I generalize on each of these points – local variations may occur and these are picked up in the text of the chapter as a whole):

- You, as a student, will have more input into the process than is common in other forms of university study (e.g. it is most likely that the decision on submission for examination is yours – within the rules of the university regarding time frames and following the guidance of your supervisors on the matter).
- Your examination will be organized for you individually (e.g. there will not be an examination room with a number of candidates in it being examined simultaneously).
- You will be allowed to take a copy of your submission into the oral examination and will be allowed to refer to it and in this sense a research degree examination is not simply a test of memory.
- The oral examination may last two hours or more and will be detailed.
- Examiners are entitled to examine you on issues related to your research as well as on what you included in your written submission (e.g. they are entitled to ask why you did not use a particular form of analysis or did not refer to a particular theorist or they may ask what alternative approaches you might have taken).
- The outcome may well be that you are awarded the degree 'subject to' amendments that the examiners will stipulate for you (this means that though the examination is 'final' it may still be followed by a period of amendment or revision).
- The examination is usually seen as being in two parts, the submission of the written work and the oral examination of you upon that work (typically you have to pass both parts to be successful).
- The result is usually indicated immediately following the oral examination (properly, the examiners will tell you what they are going to recommend to the university research degrees board or committee that acts as the examination board in these cases).

Typical processes and procedures of submission for assessment

Variations in procedures across the sector

I have headed this section as 'typical processes and procedures' because clearly all institutions will have their own procedures and within those individual departments will often have accepted custom and practice with regard to, for example, the binding of theses and to whom submission is made. Universities vary not only in their regulations in these matters but also in the amount of variation that exists within the university – some operate an almost federal system wherein individual departments, schools, faculties or institutes have considerable delegated powers to deal with the submission of research degree work and its examination. It is important then that you read the rules as they apply to you. The significance of all this to you as a research student relates back to the issues raised at the opening of this book, namely that you have a much stronger responsibility at this stage than you will ever have had as a student at taught degree level.

Task: your responsibilities in the examination process
- Check out the regulations for your particular research degree award (they will most probably be in your student handbook).
- Make a list of your responsibilities in the examination process.
- If there are any responsibilities that you are not sure of, discuss with your supervisor at a convenient opportunity (but don't leave it too late).

I wasn't going to do this task because I thought it was probably unnecessary in my case. But I went to a seminar run by the Graduate Office and after that I thought I should read through the regulations – the first time I think I have ever done that. Anyway I was surprised at just how much responsibility I do in fact have. My supervisor hadn't said any of it to me. So, it was just as well that I looked; I started filling in forms pretty well straight away. I felt a bit more in control and in the end I think the whole examination business was better than I thought. I can see that my university is very careful about giving out doctorates and, now I've got one, I appreciate that.

(Bio scientist having successfully completed a PhD)

The making of examination arrangements

There will usually be a procedure for the making of examination arrangements that involves an application to set up the arrangements being made to a committee at departmental or university level. The level of input to this procedure from you as the candidate will vary according to institution, but at the very least you will probably have to sign a document to confirm that the work to be submitted is your own and that it follows ethical guidelines and so on. In many institutions you will have some input into the choice of examiners even if this is at an informal level. For example, you may be asked if you have had any contact with potential examiners above and beyond the usual academic contact at conferences.

Prior contact with examiners

This issue of prior contact is important because if there is any contact of this kind then my advice would be that you make this absolutely clear at the outset. What you do not want is to be examined by somebody you know at a personal or professional level that falls outside of the normal academic acquaintance and which then becomes apparent either at the viva or later. Again, without wishing to sound threatening, your award is in danger if any discrepancies in this respect occur.

It is worth trying to identify at this point where the line comes when deciding if prior contact is acceptable or not. The first thing to note is that internal examiners are typically treated differently in this respect, there being a general acceptance that you may know them quite well. But, accepting this familiarity through proximity, the line comes (and this, to me, applies to potential internal and external examiners alike) when an academic has some kind of input into your own research that is more than coincidental comment and becomes more of a direct involvement in the development of your research programme. It might well be acceptable for an academic who is a potential examiner to say, 'The results you have are useful and it would be interesting to know what would have happened if you had changed variable x and re-ran the tests'; it might *not* be acceptable if that potential examiner went on to say, 'If you want to try out my suggestion I would be happy to look at your new results and run them through my own analyses'. As a very general rule then, comment is acceptable but direct involvement in the development of research is not. The reason here is, of course, that direct involvement from a potential examiner means that later, if that person becomes an examiner proper, he or she is then effectively examining their own work (inasmuch as that person has directly influenced the direction of the project).

I am devoting some space to what may seem to you an unlikely set of circumstances but in my own experience as chair of a university research degrees board, the question as to proper level of detachment of examiners came up on a number of occasions. Your university will most probably err on the side of caution because it will want to be scrupulous in its fairness to all and because involvement in the research itself, from an examiner, muddies the assessment waters mightily. This is not to say that involvement from an examiner in your work will necessarily lead to a positive outcome for you as the candidate; it may well be that the examiner thinks, 'This candidate has ignored my advice and the results are therefore dubious'. What you must always do is to be as honest and transparent as you can be whenever the issue of prior contact comes up. It is better to note for the record a connection, however tenuous, and let the committee in turn accept and note it than try to hide or obscure it in any way. Let the university committee take the strain of deciding on the substance of any grey areas that may exist; after all that is what it is there for. You do not necessarily have to resolve things such as this; you simply have to note them for others to decide upon.

Balance between subject expertise and examining experience on the examining panel

Your university will want to ensure that the examination team has adequate knowledge and specific expertise among it and also that it has the necessary experience of examining at the level that is relevant (be that masters, MPhil or doctoral). Most universities will not allow an examination to take place unless the examination team has, among its membership, some minimum of experience at the required level (regardless of how much subject knowledge the team may have among its members). There is after all a difference between knowing subject matter and research methodology and knowing about academic standards. Any attempt to fudge the amount of experience of examining necessary in the instance of an individual examination (e.g. by claiming that this is a 'new area' where little experience of examining at doctoral level exists) runs the risk of an unfair assessment occurring. Because of all this, examining research degrees is done by teams that must contain someone who is able, from previous experience, to judge whether or not a submission and the candidate's defence of it meet the criteria for the award and are therefore 'above the line' in terms of assessment for the award. The upshot of this is that, while it may seem to you that the procedures for appointing an examination team are cumbersome and overly attentive to detail, you need to realize that the university is trying to ensure that not only its standards are upheld (which is in your long-term interests inasmuch as the currency of your award, when achieved, would be in danger if those standards were allowed to slip in any way) but also you as a candidate are assured of a fair and proper assessment of your research work and your abilities as a researcher.

Making initial contact with examiners

It is usually the case that your supervisors will identify potential examiners and make an initial, informal approach to them. Typically supervisors will describe their student's research in broad outline and ask if the potential examiner would, in principle, be prepared to examine the work and the candidate in question. Universities differ in the way they handle this informal stage (there may be levels of intermediary in the process) and you need to discuss the processes with your supervisor and with relevant research tutors. As a general rule you would be advised to assume that you have no direct role in this process. You may be asked to clarify if you have prior knowledge of, and more importantly, prior contact with the potential examiner for reasons given above. At doctoral level some supervisors may operate on the basis that you may have a view as to the appropriateness of particular examiners; after all you should be conversant with key players in the scene and should be aware of researchers who would be familiar with the issues you have investigated. But, whatever the inclination of your supervisors in this respect, it is a commonly held view that ultimately it is the university that decides who should examine its research degree candidates, not the candidates themselves. Again, you will recognize the quality control issues here.

If you have any disability then it should be made known to the examiners when they are first approached to accept the appointment.

Period between approval of examination arrangements and examination itself

When the appropriate committees (there will often be a local committee that considers and then forwards for approval to a university level 'senior' committee) have finally approved you will be told by formal letter. Usually, when arrangements have been made they cannot be changed (without reference to committees that considered and approved the application in the first place) but they can stay in place for a stipulated period of time while you finalize and submit the work. Here again there are institutional differences, with some institutions allowing arrangements to be made only when the submission is ready for examination while others (more commonly) allow the arrangements to be made prior to final completion of the work so that they are in place when the final submission is made.

Submitting your work for assessment

Regulations regarding the submission that protect you as candidate

Your submission must comply with the regulations as set down by your university. Whether or not you like this, the fact is that regulations will have been written for some purpose and usually they are set out in such a way as to ensure transparency of procedures and fairness. In a sense they are there to protect you as a candidate in that any irregularity may leave you vulnerable to one form of risk or another. For example, having only one point of contact who is allowed to formally accept your work for examination, and who will give you a receipt for it, may seem overly bureaucratic but it is designed to ensure that the work actually gets into the administrative system and is then dealt with appropriately. Simply giving your dissertation to a supervisor to hand in for you when he or she is 'next in the office' or handing it over to someone who just happens to be standing in a graduate office and who looks official is, in my view, a recipe for disaster. Similarly, requiring a set number of copies in adequate temporary binding with no loose sheets is necessary if the university is to ensure that your various examiners assess the same work (if examiners do not all receive the same number of pages in the same order then the exam is likely to be unfair to you (and to them) and is likely to be declared null and void). On this point you should always make sure that all copies of the submission have the same page numbering and similarly with your own copy that you intend to take in with you to the oral examination. Examiners are quite likely to refer to specific pages – especially when looking at particular things such as figures and graphs. This is a trivial matter at one level but it takes on great significance when the candidate has to spend the entire viva translating the page numbers being cited to them to those in their own version.

Usually, when a research degree submission has been made then no further changes or amendments can be made in advance of the oral examination. If you do find errors of whatever kind between the time when you submit and the time of the viva then you should make a clear note of them and take them into the viva with you, effectively as a list of errata. I will return to the issue of amendments that might be made following the viva in a later section.

Detail of the format of your submission

Within the procedures as laid down by your university for the submission of research degree work for examination there are likely to be regulations pertaining to the actual physical presentation of the work. You need to read these earlier rather than later in the process of producing your submission for assessment. The detail may well include matters of line spacing, margin width and sometimes even typeface and font size to be used; it will probably include detail of the way the title page is to be set out. It may extend to the way in which you set out references. In the writing of the submission these things will not be problematic if you have recognized and conformed as you write. If you have to go through an entire dissertation making changes then that can be extremely problematic.

Preparation for the oral examination

When you submit your work for assessment this does not mean that there is nothing more you can do until the examination. Most supervisors will recommend that before the oral examination itself you should be given a chance to rehearse what that event might be like. Opinions vary as to whether a 'mock viva' or a meeting with supervisors at which possible questions and issues are discussed is the best way of preparing you for the examination. My own view is that both approaches have advantages and disadvantages and it is a matter of personal preference for you and your supervisors as to which is likely to be the most beneficial. Whatever the form of your 'rehearsal', I identify below what the process needs to try to achieve:

- Identify the strengths and weaknesses in the methods you employed.
- Develop a discussion about the nature of your underlying thesis and how best to defend it.
- Identify the contribution made by your research.
- Identify key aspects of being a researcher that you have mastered.
- Confirm your knowledge of the associated literature and your appreciation of how the research embodied in the submission relates to it and extends it.
- Check your understanding of the analysis and presentation of your research data and findings.
- Identify any errors, omissions or ambiguities in your submission.
- Discuss the possible different formats of the oral examination and encourage you to be fully aware of the examiners' research expertise and published work.
- Stress to you that examiners are entitled to question you on all matters related to the topic of the submission – they are not restricted to what you wrote about.
- Outline the role of supervisors in the oral examination and any aftermath if that is appropriate.

Task: preparation for the viva

What do you think would be the best way for you to prepare for the real viva:

- A meeting to discuss the kinds of questions that might arise in the viva etc.?
- A mock viva at which you role play the event?

Whatever you think, discuss the matter with your supervisor.

I opted for a meeting and I guess it worked out OK. Though I did feel after the real viva that I could have done with some practice at handling the pressure of hard questions being fired at me.

(Successful EngD candidate)

I had a mock viva and at the time it felt a bit silly with my supervisor asking me questions that I knew she knew the answer to and most of the questions she asked me at the mock did not come up anyway . . . but nevertheless it was useful, if only in giving me confidence when she said she thought I handled the mock well.

(Successful DBA candidate)

Assessment of your written submission and of you as a research degree candidate

Approaches taken by examiners to the assessment of your written work

When examiners sit down to read your submitted work they take the approach that best suits their own style of working. Some will begin from the opening pages and read sequentially through to the end. Some will glance through the appendices and references first and then go back and start to read from the beginning. Yet others will read the conclusions first and then begin to read the actual body of the text. Almost all will read the abstract fairly early in the process of reading to assess. Some will make notes directly onto your text, some will write the report as they go while others will simply note down the questions that they want to ask at the viva.

I mention all of the above variations to emphasize to you that when you construct your submission you need to bear in mind that your readers will not all begin at the beginning and read sequentially through and hence you need to have structured your work so that it can be accessed in any one of these ways; furthermore, when you are being examined orally you face people who will have come to your work differently and whose style of questioning will reflect the way in which they approached the task. Some may choose to begin with global questions and then pick out specific points. Some may ask first about your conclusions and then proceed to unpick your justifications for them. All require a response from you. I will return to these things in following sections.

What examiners look for in your written submission

When they read your work examiners should be looking to see if you have met the criteria for the award as set out in your university's regulations. The evidence is however that this is not always the case. Examiners tend to bring to the examination of a research degree their own ideas about what the various research degree awards mean in terms of level and purpose. For example, some will interpret a doctorate as primarily a research training and others will see it as an award granted when an identifiable contribution to knowledge has been made. The former may be primarily interested in you and what you have learnt as a researcher while the latter may focus upon what you found during your research and will want to judge its significance and originality as a contribution. Of course these types are not mutually exclusive – many examiners will incorporate both notions in their judgement making and in their questioning of you. I set out the styles as above merely to indicate the range of interpretations that faces you and to which you need to be able to respond.

Approaches that examiners take to oral questioning

Examiners take differing approaches to the way in which they set about questioning you on your work. If I use the same crude dichotomy as in the above section then I can extrapolate that those examiners who interpret the award as a training in research will focus their questioning upon what you have learnt from doing the research. Indeed, such an examiner might start by asking directly what you think you have learnt from doing your research. At the other end of the interpretive continuum, an examiner who sees the award as indicating the making of a contribution to knowledge may well focus on, for example, the reliability, significance and originality of what you claim to have contributed.

You may be thinking that all of this might amount to the same kind of thing in terms of actual questions asked and of course there would be some truth in this. All kinds of examiners will end up asking about how well you understand what you have done and what you have found out and what the implications are for other researchers who might wish to take your work further or take it in different directions. My point is, however, that it helps to know that examiners may be coming to their task from different directions and hence their points of focus may be different.

Style of questionning

Some examiners will assume their role to be an interrogative one and some will appear to adopt a confrontational style. This role can become an adversarial one with you and your research 'in the dock' (metaphorically speaking). That is, examiners operating on this interpretation of role will attempt to undermine the thesis that you are putting forward based on your research. Indeed, it is quite common for examiners to ask you to state what the intellectual position is that you wish to defend. Many other countries do not have a viva in the way that occurs in the UK but rather a 'defence', which is public and at which the candidate is expected formally to state his or her thesis that is then attacked by an official 'opponent' (who is generally not an examiner). In other words, at doctoral level at least there is a notion that permeates proceedings that what all are engaged in is a 'doctoral defence'.

Again, I can contrast this interrogative approach with examiners who will see their role as being to engage with the candidate in a discussion of the findings and to draw out what he or she knows as a result of engaging in the research. In such circumstances the oral examination becomes less of an interrogation and more of an exploration of ideas and findings. This approach may sound more attractive to you as a candidate but I would not wish you to fear the interrogation mode that I described earlier. 'Interrogation' may have unfortunate connotations but in the academic sense it is, to me at least, quite a reasonable way to proceed. Indeed, it may have advantages for you as a candidate because it is perhaps more transparent than a more discursive and engaging discussion that may end up unfocused.

Verification of authorship

There is one more aspect to the purpose of the oral examination, which may underpin the way the examiners approach their task, and that is the need to verify within the examination process that you as the candidate are the proper author of the work. You may find this offensive to read but it is the case that research degree submissions have been known to be partially or wholly plagiarized. It has also been the case in the broad history of research degree study that some candidates have not been wholly responsible for all of the work that is presented for submission. In the former of these two instances there can be no excuse for plagiarism and no realistic outcome (assuming the plagiarism to be significant) other than failure. However, in the latter instance (whole responsibility for the work), there may be something of a grey area. It may be for example that, as discussed in Chapter 5, the work involved collaboration with a broader research team and some data collection or analysis etc. was done by colleagues other than the candidate. It is impossible here to define rules in respect of such circumstances where judgements might clearly be made. What you need to do where such collaboration has occurred is to delineate very clearly in your written submission just where some research activity, which you need to report to substantiate your thesis, was carried out or supported by others. There are disciplinary differences here but for the most part such collaboration is most likely to be acceptable, especially in the context of cross-disciplinary studies. In short, you should always discuss any input from others into any aspect of your work with your supervisor and you should always acknowledge that input in your written submission. Finally, of course, you also need to be prepared to defend and justify it as you would any other aspect of your work.

Correction of errors

There is one dimension that is a feature of the oral examination that very often far outweighs its real importance and indeed I fear is one where custom and practice has grown beyond real purpose and stated intent. I refer here to the role that examiners play in checking and suggesting amendments to the literary worthiness of the text and to the accuracy of the way in which data are set out in ways such as the graphical and the tabular. In short, many examiners expend a considerable amount of energy in correcting the text and the general content of submissions. Again, this is in direct contrast to the situation outside of the UK (in the rest of Europe and beyond) where the dissertation as submitted is what is published (sometimes with a simple errata slip inserted) regardless of what happened at the defence, assuming that the candidate passes. There is a difference then between seeing the process of examination as including revising the text or seeing it as solely concerned with assessing the work as it is presented. In my view, the pendulum in the UK has swung too far and some oral examinations become a matter of the examiners fine tuning the literary qualities of the candidate's work. Examiners themselves will often disagree about the extent to which they should become involved in noting all typographical and more substantive grammatical and presentational errors in a dissertation. Some will arrive at the viva with a list of errors that they hand to the candidate and which then become a part of the amendments required by the examiners before the award can be made. Others arrive with only their questions and sometimes with a verbal instruction to 'sort out the typos'.

Pragmatic features of the oral examination (viva)

Asking for clarification

It is usually accepted that you as the candidate are entitled to ask for clarification if any question put to you by the examiners seems unclear. This makes the oral examination of a research degree somewhat different from the usual academic examination where you are sat in a room with no access to means of clarification and where you have to rely on your memory and unsupported interpretive faculties in order to make progress. A research degree examination is more analogous to an interview in which you are tested on what you know and what you did in your project but where that testing takes the shape of a dialogue, albeit an adversarial one. Research is a complex matter and examiners may at times struggle themselves to make clear what they are trying to probe and why. A polite request for clarification may therefore be helpful all round.

Place of supervisors at the oral examination

Whether or not supervisors are allowed to attend the oral examination, and what their subsequent role is at the event, varies across universities in the UK. Most will allow some supervisory presence but some will not; some will allow only one supervisor to be present while others will allow the team to attend; many will have some restriction on how active a role those supervisors may play in the examination; some for example will allow supervisors to attend but not with the right to speak unless asked directly by the examiners. Importantly for us here, many institutions will make attendance of supervisors a matter for the discretion of you as the candidate. In the light of this last point I will outline below the kinds of role supervisors may play and hence try to indicate the advantages of their presence for you as the candidate.

The main advantage of your supervisor attending is that you have someone else present who can listen to all comments made, make notes as the viva progresses and be in a better position to help you interpret any requirements that the examiners make of you by way of amendments. Indeed, you may well be in a temporarily confused state, of elation as much as anything else, when the examiners set about telling you what they want you to amend, if anything. You should always get their recommendations in writing later but nevertheless there is no substitute for being present and listening dispassionately to what they say, because what is said sometimes clarifies what is later set down in writing.

A second advantage for you as the candidate is that, if your institutional regulations permit it, your supervisor may be able to indicate to examiners any instances where he or she thinks you have misinterpreted a question (i.e. your supervisor knows you well enough to know that you have misinterpreted or misunderstood a specific question). In other words your supervisor may be able to act in a supportive way at the viva. I should stress that your supervisor's ability to help you in this way will always be limited (if allowed at all); he or she cannot, after all, intervene more than minimally without beginning to undermine the examination process.

Length of the oral examination

Probable length of examination varies not so much between institutions as between disciplines. Oral examinations in the sciences and engineering are on average shorter than in the arts and humanities. It would be rare for a viva to take less than an hour and equally rare for it to take more than four hours. In between these two time periods anything is possible though most oral examinations will be completed in two, or two and a half, hours. It is worth noting here that some examinations take longer because they involve some kind of practical demonstration, some include a comfort break and others involve some fairly extensive discussion after the result is announced. None of these things are necessarily negative; in my experience the viva that takes longer is not necessarily indicative of any defect in the work or the candidate but on the contrary may relate to the interest that the examiners showed in the work. For many academics (students and examiners alike) a research degree examination is one of the few chances they have to look into specific topics that are of mutual intellectual interest in some depth and for some uninterrupted time. Research seminars and papers are most often restricted to brief inputs and with little time for questions. So here in the research degree examination, for better or worse, there is an opportunity for in-depth and intensive interrogation and discussion of a research topic that should be of interest to all parties.

Likely outcomes and activities subsequent to the viva

Range of possible outcomes

As with pretty well every other section in this chapter, the range of possible outcomes from research degree examinations will vary across institutions. Again, you really need to check out your own situation in your university's regulations but I summarize below the basic levels of outcome that are usual at research degree level.

- The 'highest' level is usually 'pass' or 'pass with no amendments'. The only exception would be where an institution marks out some passes as 'pass with commendation' or with 'special merit'. In my view (possibly idiosyncratic) this kind of finer definition of pass at doctoral level specifically is both unnecessary and potential damaging to the credibility of the award because a doctorate is a signifier of excellence and hence to try to establish something as 'more excellent' (*sic*) than something else is logically implausible. There is also the danger that those who gain a doctorate that does not have the notion of merit attached to it may well feel that their award is of lesser value (and indeed it effectively becomes of lesser value). Setting aside this possible exception of commendation or special merit, a straight pass is what one would most wish for, though it is increasingly uncommon, certainly at doctoral level, where amendments of one kind or another are often seen by examiners as customary.
- The second level of success is a 'pass with amendments' and is often, though not always, further subdivided into two categories: pass with minor amendments and pass with major or substantial amendments. If you receive either one of these recommendations then it means, effectively, that you are deemed to have passed but that this pass is conditional upon you undertaking amendments to your submission as directed by the examiners and to their satisfaction and within a stated time frame. Often this checking that the work has been done 'to their satisfaction' is delegated either to one of the examiners who acts on behalf of the others or to a supervisor (usually the principal supervisor).
- The next level is where the examiners decide that the work presented to them is not adequate for the award in question or that the defence of the work was not convincing enough (or, of course, both of these things). They may then agree to recommend that the candidate be given the chance to resubmit the work for examination at a later date. Again, there are important subcategories and nuances within this broad level, perhaps most significantly where examiners may ask for the resubmission (sometimes known as a referral) to involve another viva or not. The basic point about this level is that here the candidate has not passed but the examiners have deemed that there is enough merit in the work and/or in the candidate for that candidate

to be given the chance to resubmit and be examined on that resubmission (with or without a second viva). Again, there will usually be a time limit within which the resubmission must be made. Of course, this is not the outcome that you will want but if it does happen then you need to hold on to the fact that the examiners did not think that the work was beyond hope; they are basically saying that it can be retrieved with more work of one kind or another.

- The next level (not available in all universities) is where examiners decide that the work does not merit the award for which the candidate has submitted but that it does meet the criteria for a lower award. For example, a submission and its defence might be deemed inadequate for PhD but acceptable for MPhil in that it meets the criteria for that lower award. This latter point is important because there is a common understanding here that the MPhil (or indeed any other award that is below doctoral standard) should not be used as a consolation prize – should not in effect, in the example given above, be an award that signifies a 'failed PhD'. The examiners in the example are making a positive suggestion that the work does meet the criteria for that lower award. In some universities a candidate may be given the choice, in such circumstances, between accepting the award of (in this example) MPhil or undertaking a resubmission for the award of PhD.
- The final level is where the examiners deem the work to be not of the necessary standard and further that it is not retrievable and that it does not meet the criteria for any other (lower) award. This level may be described as 'fail with no retrieval' or similar words. I should note here that this level is a very rare outcome and clearly one that you would wish to avoid.

Dealing with amendments and possible resubmission

You would be wise to undertake any amendments that you have been given with alacrity. I never ceased to be amazed at candidates who have received really quite minor amendments but who, perhaps for reasons of anti-climax following the viva, do not set about making them immediately or as soon as possible after the viva. You must remember that while the examiners have agreed to recommend that your work meets the required standard, it is also the case that this agreement is 'subject to' the amendments being made. You run the risk of never receiving the award if you do not complete the amendments as soon as you can.

On a more substantial note, if you are given amendments to complete then you are entitled to supervisory guidance as to how to attend to these. Thus supervisory attendance at the viva can prove valuable. All experienced supervisors will have encountered situations where amendments are needed and most will help you deal with them quickly and efficiently even where they themselves may feel the amendments to be unnecessary.

All of the above also extends to resubmission and re-examination. There is a sense in which your registration as a student continues through all the possible phases of being a candidate and the university should support you throughout, until the award is made or until, in extreme circumstances, your submission fails irretrievably.

Complaints and appeals

I hope that your experience of research degree study and examination will be an interesting and enjoyable one. But clearly there are occasions when things will not run as everyone concerned would wish and here the possibilities of complaining and/or appealing arise. As this chapter is focused upon the examination phase I will not refer here to any complaint you may have wished to make during your period of study except to say that all universities will have a complaints procedure and you will have been given a copy of it; most likely it will be referred to in your student handbook or similar. The examination phase is different, although clearly any complaint you might have made during your studies could have an impact at this later stage.

Your university will recognize that, with the best will in the world and with all checks and safeguards in place, there are occasions when some aspect of the judgement-making process that is made manifest through the examination fails in some respect. If you feel genuinely that your examination was unsound or improper then you have the right to appeal against the decision as to outcome that is conveyed to you by the examination board (e.g. the research degrees committee, board or senate). In phrasing the previous sentence in the way that I have, I am noting that usually you cannot appeal until the awarding committee has passed its decision to you; as you will recall the examiners merely recommend an outcome to that board.

You must, of course, have some basis for appealing against the outcome and typically the published appeals procedure in your institution will frame some set 'grounds for appeal' within which you must fix your own appeal. Typically, these grounds will encompass mismanagement of the examination process such that you were not given a fair and reasonable chance to present and defend your work to the best of your ability, circumstances that impinged upon the examination process and of which you were not able to make the examiners aware and unfair or improper assessment by one or more of the examiners. Lack of space prevents me from going into all of these possibilities in detail and, in any case, it would be extremely rarely that you would ever need to be aware of them and to explore their possibilities. The broad advice must be that if you find yourself in a position of needing to appeal against an examination outcome then read the appeals procedure, seek advice from student representatives and act properly within the rules.

Summary

- You have considered the way in which research degrees are examined in the UK and have, to a small degree, compared that with the situation elsewhere; your purpose has been to understand the process well enough to make the most out of the opportunities offered by the process of examination.
- You have considered processes and procedures of research degree examination as well as custom and practice in the UK.
- You have thought about what is involved in the judgement making as it relates to your written submission and indeed to your strengths as a candidate.
- You have considered the academic and institutional purposes of the oral examination (viva).
- You have thought about the likely pragmatic features of the examination and the possible outcomes of your examination.
- You have reflected on the various things that follow the recommendations that arise from the viva (e.g. amendments to written submission).

Conclusion

I have ended the main text of this chapter on a rather negative note in discussing the possibilities of appealing and complaining. This is unfortunate in that I would not wish to leave you with the impression that the experience of being examined at research degree level is likely to be an unpleasant or negative one. In most cases this is most certainly not how things are experienced by candidates. Indeed, many research degree students will look back on their viva as a high spot in their intellectual lives. It is an occasion when you have the chance to discuss your research in some detail, to debate the questions you have sought to answer and those your work has raised. Of course it may be challenging but that challenge is what you should want out of your research studies. The point is to meet the challenge and overcome it and I hope that reading this chapter will have gone some way to helping you to achieve that. To return full circle to the sentiments in the quotation from Joubert with which I opened this chapter, I hope that you will feel the need to debate the questions and indeed that it would be unsatisfying to settle your work without such debate.

11

Conclusion

Overview • Introduction • Maintaining focus in the face of risk and variable progress • The reflective practitioner • Support from supplementary reading • Self-doubt, uncertainty and challenge • Summary • Conclusion

'Cheshire-Puss,' she began, rather timidly . . . 'Would you tell me, please, which way I ought to go from here?'
'That depends a good deal on where you want to get to,' said the cat.
'I don't much care where . . . ,' said Alice.
'Then it doesn't matter which way you go,' said the cat.
> Lewis Carroll (1832–1898), *Alice's Adventures in Wonderland* (1865)

Overview

In this chapter I will draw together what has gone before in the book and return full circle to the issue of how you may interpret returning to study in particular and ways of learning in general that I raised in Chapters 1 and 2. In this chapter, therefore, you will be asked to:

- reconsider your reasons for returning to study (and for a research degree in particular) and set these in the context of needing to persevere with your studies
- think about the way in which rates of progress in both academic study and research terms are likely to vary

- consider how the concept of reflective practice, and in particular its relationship to research, may relate to you
- reflect upon how academic study in general, and research work as part of that study in particular, involves you in taking risks, which may, in turn, impact upon your own professional development where appropriate.

Introduction

Advice as to the direction to be taken is dependent on where the questioner wishes to go, as the Cheshire Puss is at pains to point out to Alice in the quote at the start of this chapter. Similarly, as a student returning to study at research degree level, it is important that you develop an understanding of where you want your studying and your researching to lead. Seeking strategies to maintain your progress as a researcher and making use of the various kinds of available support are all contingent upon your goals.

For some readers the return to study is, in part at least, a matter of needing further professional qualifications and I have already discussed the way in which researching may well be seen as the highest level of academic study as it relates to the professions. However, it is most probably an oversimplification to suggest that you are engaging with your current, or proposed, programme of research study simply because you need further (professional) qualifications. While such things may be driving your decision making at one level there may well be a variety of reasons, both personal and professional, that also come into the equation and an honest appraisal of all of your goals and the way in which they interrelate may help you to manage your research study effectively.

Research is an activity that naturally attracts many people because it allows an engagement with the creation of knowledge as well as the (mere) accumulation of existing knowledge. In my view, you should not be shy of laying claim to that attraction. In some strands of society there is an anti-intellectual attitude that seeks to diminish the value of wanting to understand things better and wanting at the same time to influence the way in which others can come to see the world. As a researcher you need to resist such attitudes. Without wishing to sound overly pompous, any liberal society needs some of its members to be working at the edges of understanding and to push back boundaries; your research studies are part of the realization of that need.

Maintaining focus in the face of risk and variable progress

Perseverance

I would not wish this book to end on a pessimistic note but it is sobering to recognize that a significant proportion of students who return to study at research degree level do not complete their chosen programme of research work for one reason or another. Indeed, it is likely that more than one reason will combine in individual cases to provoke lack of completion. I have used the phrase 'lack of completion' here because, in my experience, those who do not succeed in gaining the award will have withdrawn themselves rather than have failed through any process of assessment. You will have noted in Chapter 10 that it is rare for a candidate who has submitted for a research degree to fail outright but as a corollary to that I must note that the submission rate for returning students is less than optimistic.

This is not to suggest of course that only those of you who are prepared to persevere with your programme of research study will succeed, but rather that there are features in life that may conspire to foil an honest and enthusiastic attempt at returning to study. In short, life happens. It would be facile to try to list here the aspects of your personal and/or professional life that might affect your progress as a research student significantly; suffice to say that they exist for the vast majority of returning students. It may be opportune for you to think back to your reading of Chapter 1 when you were asked to consider your reasons for returning to study. Some of my own students have found that when they have needed to take difficult decisions, as a result of various life changes for example, then they have had to strike a balance between the continuing relevance of their initial reasons and conflicts that have arisen during their time of research degree study.

Of course, an alternative approach to the above notions of perseverance would be to follow the advice (not recommended here but noted nonetheless) of W.C. Fields, 'If at first you don't succeed, try, try, again. Then quit. No use being a damned fool about it.'

Risk taking

There is a natural tension between, first, the need for some kind of surety that the research programme, with its methodologies and procedures, will end up with research findings that will meet adequately the criteria for the award to which the student is aiming, second, the need for that student to learn about researching (and in a way that is evidential), and third, the need for the research itself to engage with the unknown and the uncertain and the significant. In short, all concerned want the programme of research to be robust and safe enough to produce a 'result', yet most will accept that all research necessarily involves some risk inasmuch as it needs to challenge the known and explore the unknown. Of course, it is the case that we can make research programmes 'safer' by making sure that they conform to the necessary rules and accepted procedures that apply within the discipline and in this way an acceptable result does not have to be a positive finding. It may well be, for example, that your research clarifies issues in certain practical investigations that enable others to go on and make significant strides in terms of discoveries of one sort or another. In this sense, a 'negative' result should always tell you as the researcher something. But however one qualifies and reassures, I think that the tension that I note above persists. In the domain of research degree training, you as a student learn to be a researcher through doing research and by reporting what you have done and what you have learnt through that process. The process is one that therefore involves the unknown and that in turn is synonymous with the uncertain.

Task: risk taking within your research
Draw up a bullet point list of risks inherent in your research.

What can you do (or have you done) to

- recognize the risk
- seek to minimize it?

There were in fact various risks in my research programme. Some were kind of practical like not being able to find enough subjects (in my case young adults with schizophrenia) but another, more serious, was that the questionnaire I devised might not be sensitive enough to get worthwhile information from this volatile group. I suppose our answer to this was to include in the programme some in-depth interviews, case studies and observations. In the end the study was much richer than it would have been if I had put all my energies into the questionnaire alone – which had been my original intention.

(Successful DClinPsy student)

Rate of progress

I have seen many of my own research students become frustrated when progress on their chosen research programme seems to them to be unnaturally slow. Yet I think it needs to be recognized that rate of progress in research in general, and perhaps particularly in research study, will tend to be irregular. Real research is typified by periods of trial and testing that are in an immediate sense non-productive and these can be set against contrasting times when things come together and 'results' arise seemingly freely. Also, there are typically learning curves where you may find yourself spending some time mastering a particular technique or reading around a topic before your efforts begin to engage with research activity and later produce findings or results. If you come from a professional background then you might contrast this phenomenon with your professional work where the relationship between effort and progress may seem more regular and therefore more predictable (clearly, I am not implying that there is never a gap between effort and result; indeed it may be a feature of your particular professional background that considerable background work has to be completed before things become clearer and efforts can come to fruition). Frequently, it is the unfamiliarity of rate of progress in academic research work that can be unnerving for those returning to study and you may have to rationalize what is happening in this respect.

Reflection: rates of progress
- Can you think of examples from your previous experiences of study, or from your current professional practice, in which there has been a signifi- cant amount of time and effort expended before any real gains in terms of production or of new learning of knowledge or skills?
- How justifiable does the time and effort seem now, in retrospect?

I do a lot of background work before finalizing suggestions on a project. It is still a necessary expense of time, although I am better now at judging how complex a presentation a client needs. Without the background work a project is likely to lack depth – in some ways I hate to work on things that won't really feature in the final presentation but at the same time I know it is necessary. I guess it's the same with academic work although I confess that there I am likely to plunge in without the background. Maybe I need to learn a lesson.

(Designer enrolled for a DArt)

I spent ages getting into using the stats package my supervisor recom- mended but now I understand it and what it does I am beginning to see the possibilities. I realized fairly early on that I simply cannot get on with the practical things I want to do until I have mastered how I am going to analyse all the data. I am a practical person and I want to get on and test out some ideas I have developed back at work but I need the grounding first so I know how to set up my testing.

(Engineer at the end of the first Year of an EngD programme)

The reflective practitioner

If you came to your studies from a professional background or from some setting in which you might be described as a 'practitioner', yours may be one of the many professions that currently make use of the concept of a 'reflective practitioner'. As professions have developed and as society has become more complex, then the notion of a set body of knowledge, learnt once and adequate for the purpose throughout a career, has changed. It is likely that, as a professional engaged in research degree study, you need to see yourself as working effectively at your practice, improving your professional skills and enhancing your knowledge base within that practice, and learning to use research as an integral part of your practice (both as a consumer of the research findings of others and as an active researcher yourself). In many ways it may no longer be good enough to be able to perform at an adequate level of professional practice in the here and now – you may also have to monitor continuously your professional processes with a view to improvement in all three of these levels I describe above.

Typically, within research degree study, issues within professional practice that need to be investigated and evaluated are identified, ways of systematically analysing practice are explored and the implications of any modifications to that practice are discussed. What is required from you out of all of this is change to your professional practice that is based on reasoned argument, research investigations and resulting evidence and which results in a 'better' situation (you may wish to reflect on what could count as 'better' in your own professional context, though one could argue that it should, in one way or another, relate ultimately to improvement for the client group). Of course the above scenario is cyclical: change will bring about circumstances that in themselves need to be open to scrutiny and so the cycle of reflection, research, action and change will continue.

I do think that all of us involved in research degree study need to question who or what the intended beneficiaries of our reflective practice and research are and we need to make judgements about the real as opposed to imaginary benefits in this respect. One student (a graphic designer) when discussing this point commented in a more or less positive vein:

> It is very important for me to redefine my concept of what a graphic designer is, because that concept is always changing from day to day, because of the medium of technology I use. (The variety of work I do incorporates illustration, graphic design, concept design, project and marketing design.) The rhetoric on my initial training course was that, 'you now know everything that there is to know to be a graphic designer' – but it was just the tip of the iceberg. I now realize, through doing research, that I need to rethink that stance so that I conceive of myself as a designer

who has some of the tools that enable me to change the way we see design and what it can do for all of us – well, for the clients at least.

Support from supplementary reading

Throughout this book I have mentioned sources in the literature where you may find help on certain issues and this is perhaps the moment to draw your attention again to the Further Reading offered at the end of this book. The 11 sections included there cover a range of topics and at this point it seems reasonable to suggest that it might be profitable if you skimmed through the titles listed, reading more widely as you see fit.

Self-doubt, uncertainty and challenge

It would be glib at this stage of the book for me to suggest simply that self-doubt is a perfectly normal and acceptable feature of returning to study, particularly perhaps at research degree level. I accept that doubting one's own abilities can be a destructive force if, for example, it results in a concentration on defence against perceived threat rather than a focus on learning (e.g. *'It's all very well of my supervisor to say that I should have written in a more robust style in my conclusion – she did not have to write it under the kinds of pressure that I had at the time'*, rather than *'I wonder just how I could have been more robust in my writing without appearing to claim too much from my data?'*). But I have to say that self-doubt is common among many of those I have known who have returned to study for a research degree and indeed it is prevalent among many of those who spend the majority of their professional lives within academia.

It seems to me that there is a sense in which, when you engage in study through research, necessarily you challenge yourself and your beliefs and that with that challenge come the attendant risks of doubting your beliefs, your knowledge systems and indeed, where applicable, the effectiveness of your own professional skills. In short, constant critical evaluation of your own professional practice can seem inevitably to provoke uncertainty. But I want to end this book on an optimistic note because I feel that returning to study for a research degree should be an enriching and, if it does not sound too pious, a life-enhancing experience. For my part I have come to accept that uncertainty, while it may be uncomfortable, is a more natural, and ultimately more beneficial, state of mind than certainty. Voltaire put this succinctly when he wrote that, 'Doubt is not a pleasant condition, but certainty is absurd'.

Summary

- You have considered personal interpretations of returning to study and ways of learning.
- You have reconsidered your reasons for returning to study at research degree level.
- You have addressed issues relating to the way in which rates of progress in research and in study about research are likely to vary.
- You have considered the concept of the reflective practitioner and any impact it may have if you are a professional who is learning to use research in your work.
- You have thought about the inevitability of risk taking in academic study.
- You have reflected on the value of uncertainty and challenge as a credo.

Conclusion

There is a tension of sorts between the way the words of Lewis Carroll are employed at the outset of this chapter, and the kind of acceptance of uncertainty advocated at the end. On the one hand the usefulness of knowing where you are going is stressed and yet on the other the foolhardiness of accepting certainty is underlined. How then can I ask you to reconcile the need for a clear sense of direction with a rejection of certainty? It seems to me that the answer needs to be worked through by you at the level of defining, for yourself, the personal and professional goals that you wish to attain. This will involve you in questioning accepted wisdoms within your professional field and your own assumptions about: your ways of learning, your developing abilities as a researcher and your motivation in making the doing of research an inevitable part of your life. A response to the Cheshire Puss (that is, to the question *'Where do you want to get to?'*), in the context of returning to study for a research degree, might be that you wish to get to a situation where you are more able to ask the right questions within your professional work, know how to use research methods that will yield useful answers to those questions and understand better the questions and answers of others in the field.

The exciting thing about returning to study for a research degree is that it gives you the opportunity to challenge accepted views and rethink your own ideas as well as to develop any professional knowledge and skills you may have and enhance your personal abilities as a thinker and a learner. My hope is that reading this book will help you to take that opportunity and exploit it to the full.

Further reading

The following books and articles may prove useful in your return to study at research degree level. I have separated them into sections for convenience though clearly there is some overlap. The early sections relate to research degree students and study specifically, whereas later sections include texts that relate to academic study more generally.

1 General guidance for research students

Bentley, P.J. (2006) *The PhD Application Handbook*. Maidenhead: Open University Press.

Cryer, P. (1996) *The Research Student's Guide to Success*. Buckingham: Open University Press.

Elphinstone, L. and Schweitzer, R. (1998) *How to Get a Research Degree: A Survival Guide*. St Leonards, Australia: Allen and Unwin.

Leonard, D. (2001) *A Woman's Guide to Doctoral Studies*. Buckingham: Open University Press.

Longman, J. and Hall, G. (eds) (2008) *The Research Student's Companion*. London: Sage.

Phillips, E.M. and Pugh, D.S. (2005) *How to Get a PhD: A Handbook for Students and their Supervisors*. Maidenhead: Open University Press.

Potter, S. (ed.) (2006) *Doing Postgraduate Research*. Maidenhead: Open University Press with Sage.

Rugg, G. and Petre, M. (2004) *The Unwritten Rules of PhD Research*. Maidenhead: Open University Press.

Wright, J. and Lodwick, R. (1989) The process of the PhD: a study of the first year of doctoral study. *Research Papers in Education*, 4: 22–56.

2 Research study skills and methods

Bell, J. (2005) *Doing your Research Project: A Guide for First-time Researchers in Education and Social Science*. Maidenhead: Open University Press.

Blaxter, L., Hughes, C. and Tight, M. (2006) *How to Research*. Maidenhead: Open University Press.

Denscombe, M. (2007) *The Good Research Guide for Small-Scale Social Research Projects.* Maidenhead: Open University Press.

Gillham, B. (2005) *Research Interviewing: The Range of Techniques.* Maidenhead: Open University Press.

Hamp-Lyons, L. and Courter, K.B. (1984) *Research Matters.* New York: Harper & Row.

Keats, D. (2000) *Interviewing.* Buckingham: Open University Press.

Oliver, P. (2003) *The Student's Guide to Research Ethics.* Maidenhead: Open University Press.

Orna, L. (1995) *Managing Information for Research.* Buckingham: Open University Press.

Rugg, G. (2007) *Using Statistics: A Gentle Introduction.* Maidenhead: Open University Press.

Rugg, G. and Petre, M. (2006) *A Gentle Guide to Research Methods.* Maidenhead: Open University Press.

3 Academic writing about research

Booth, V. (1993) *Communicating in Science: Writing a Scientific Paper and Speaking at Scientific Meetings,* 2nd edn. Cambridge: Cambridge University Press.

Canter, D. and Fairbairn, G. (2006) *Becoming an Author: Advice for Academics and Other Professionals.* Maidenhead: Open University Press.

Collinson, D., Kirkup, G., Kyd, R. and Slocombe, L. (1992) *Plain English.* Buckingham: Open University Press.

Day, R.A. (1989) *How to Write and Publish a Scientific Paper,* 3rd edn. Cambridge: Cambridge University Press.

Fairbairn, G.J. and Winch, C. (1996) *Reading, Writing and Reasoning: A Guide for Students,* 2nd edn. Buckingham: Open University Press.

Hers, H.G. (1984) Making science a good read. *Nature, 307:* 205.

Lobban, C.S. and Schefter, M. (1993) *Successful Lab Reports: A Manual for Science Students.* Cambridge: Cambridge University Press.

Miller, C. and Swift, K. (1989) *The Handbook of Non-sexist Writing: For Writers, Editors and Speakers,* 2nd edn. London: The Womens Press.

Murray, R. (2004) *Writing for Academic Journals.* Maidenhead: Open University Press.

Murray, R. (2006) *How to Write a Thesis.* Maidenhead: Open University Press.

Sides, C.H. (1992) *How to Write and Present Technical Information,* 2nd edn. Cambridge: Cambridge University Press.

Swales, J. (1990) *Genre Analysis: English in Academic and Research Settings.* New York: Cambridge University Press.

Swales, J.M. and Feak, C.B. (1994) *Academic Writing for Graduate Students.* Ann Arbor, MI: University of Michigan Press.

Torrance, M.S. and Thomas, G.V. (1994) The development of writing skills in doctoral research students, in R.G. Burgess (ed.) *Postgraduate Education and Training in the Social Sciences: Processes and Products.* London: Jessica Kingsley.

Weissberg, R. and Buker, S. (1990) *Writing up Research: Experimental Research Report Writing for Students of English.* Englewood Cliffs, NJ: Prentice-Hall.

Zinsser, W. (1985) *On Writing Well: An Informal Guide to Writing Non-fiction,* 3rd edn. New York: Harper & Row.

4 Oral research presentations

Allison, D. and Bramwell, N. (1994) It'll be all right on the day. *Biologist, 41*: 4 (note: this is a short article on giving oral presentations and is not subject specific).

Norris, J.R. (1978) How to give a research talk: notes for inexperienced lecturers. *Biologist, 25*: 68–74.

5 Research degree supervision (including publications directed at supervisors)

Black, D. (1994) *A Guide for Research Supervisors*. Dereham, UK: Peter Francis.

Brockbank, A. and McGill, I. (1998) *Facilitating Reflective Learning in Higher Education*. Buckingham: Open University Press.

Delamont, S., Atkinson P. and Parry, O. (1997) *Supervising the PhD: A Guide to Success*. Buckingham: Society for Research into Higher Education (SRHE) and Open University Press.

Hockey, J. (1994) Establishing boundaries: problems and solutions in managing the PhD supervisor's role. *Cambridge Journal of Education, 24*: 293–307 (note: there are also two 'responses' to this article in the same edition of the *Cambridge Journal of Education*).

Wisker, G. (2005) *The Good Supervisor*. Basingstoke: Palgrave Macmillan.

6 Research degree examination (including publications directed at examiners)

Pearce, L. (2005) *How to Examine a Thesis*. Maidenhead: SRHE and Open University Press.

Powell, S.D. and Brown, K. (2007) *Accessibility of PhD Examiners' Reports*. Lichfield, UK: UK Council for Graduate Education.

Powell, S.D. and Green, H. (2003) Research degree examining: quality issues of principle and practice. *Quality Assurance in Education* (special edition: 'Assessing and Examining Research Awards'), 11(2): 55–64.

Powell, S.D. and Green, H. (2005) *Confidentiality in Doctoral Theses*. Lichfield, UK: UK Council for Graduate Education.

Powell, S.D. and McCauley, C. (2002) Research degree examining: common principles and divergent practices. *Quality Assurance in Education* (special edition: 'Standards and the Doctoral Award'), 10(2): 104–116.

Powell, S.D. and McCauley, C. (2003) The process of examining research degrees: some issues of quality. *Quality Assurance in Education* (special edition: 'Assessing and Examining Research Awards'), 11(2): 73–84.

Tinkler, P. and Jackson, C. (2004) *The Doctoral Examination Process: A Handbook for Students, Examiners and Supervisors*. Maidenhead: Open University Press.

7 Policy issues relating to research degree study

Green, H. and Powell, S.D. (2005) *Doctoral Study in Contemporary Higher Education*. Maidenhead: Open University Press.

Hinchcliffe, R., Bromley, T. and Hutchinson, S. (eds) (2007) *Skills Training in Research Degree Programmes: Politics and Practice*. London: McGraw-Hill.

Powell, S.D. (ed.) (2003) *Special Teaching in Higher Education: Successful Strategies for Access and Inclusion*. London: Kogan Page.

Powell, S.D. (2004) *The Award of PhD by Published Work in the UK*. Lichfield, UK: UK Council for Graduate Education.

Powell, S.D. and Green, H. (2006) The national funding of doctoral training: warnings from the English experience, *Journal of Higher Education Policy and Management, 28*(3): 263–275.

Powell, S.D. and Green, H. (2007a) A framework for the future of doctoral study: resolving inconsistent practices and incorporating innovative possibilities, in R. Hinchcliffe, T. Bromley and S. Hutchinson (eds) *Skills Training in Research Degree Programmes: Politics and Practice*. London: McGraw-Hill.

Powell, S.D. and Green, H. (2007b) *The Doctorate Worldwide*. Maidenhead: Open University Press.

Powell, S.D. and Green, H. (2008) What is a postgraduate research degree?, in J. Longman and G. Hall (eds) *The Research Student's Companion*. London: Sage.

Powell, S.D. and Long, E. (2005) *Professional Doctorate Awards in the UK*. Lichfield, UK: UK Council for Graduate Education.

Scott, D., Brown, A., Lunt, L. and Thorne, L. (2004) *Professional Doctorates: Integrating Professional and Academic Knowledge*. Maidenhead: SRHE and Open University Press.

8 General academic study guides

Arksey, H., Marchant, I. and Simmill, C. (1994) *Juggling for a Degree: Mature Students' Experience of University Life*. Lancaster: Unit for Innovation in Higher Education.

Gatrell, C. (2006) *Managing Part-time Study: A Guide for Undergraduates and Postgraduates*. Maidenhead: Open University Press.

Hampson, L. (1994) *How's your Dissertation Going?* Lancaster: Unit for Innovation in Higher Education.

Marshall, L. and Rowland, F. (1993) *A Guide to Learning Independently*, 2nd edn. Buckingham: Open University Press.

Mullarkey, N. (1993) *You Do Not Seem to Have Understood the Question*. Lancaster: University of Lancaster Press.

Northedge, A. (1990) *The Good Study Guide*. Milton Keynes: Open University Press.

Powell, S.D. (1999) *Return to Study: A Guide for Professionals*. Buckingham: Open University Press.

Pritchard, L. and Roberts, L. (2006) *The Mature Student's Guide to Higher Education*. Maidenhead: Open University Press.

Raaheim, K., Wankowski, J. and Radford, J. (1991) *Helping Students to Learn*. Milton Keynes: SRHE and Open University Press.

Race, P. (1998) *How to Get a Good Degree: Making the Most of your Time at University*. Buckingham: Open University Press.

Rickards, T. (1992) *How to Win as a Mature Student*. London: Kogan Page.

Smith, B.R. (1983) Learning difficulties of part-time mature students. *Journal of Further and Higher Education*, 7: 81–85.

9 Critical thinking

Halpern, D.F. (2003) *Thought and Knowledge: An Introduction to Critical Thinking*. Hillsdale, NJ: Lawrence Erlbaum Associates.

hooks, b. (1994) *Teaching to Transgress: Education as the Practice of Freedom*. New York: Routledge.

Meltzer, M. and Palau, S. (1996) *Acquiring Critical Thinking Skills*. London: W.B. Saunders.

Parnes, S.J., Noller, R.B. and Biondi, A.M. (1977) *Guide to Creative Action: Revised Edition of Creative Behavior Guidebook*. New York: Scribner.

Phelan, P.D. and Reynolds, P. (1995) *Argument and Evidence: Critical Thinking for the Social Sciences*. London: Routledge.

Mezirow, J. (1990) *Fostering Critical Reflection in Adulthood: A Guide to Transformative and Emancipatory Learning*. San Francisco, CA: Jossey-Bass.

10 Accessing the Internet

Hardie, E.T.L. and Neou, V. (eds) (1994) *Internet: Mailing Lists*. Englewood Cliffs, NJ: Prentice Hall.

Harmon, C. (ed.) (1996) *Using the Internet, On-line Services and CD-ROMS for Writing Research and Term Papers*. New York: Neal-Schuman.

11 General issues in higher education

Blaxter, L., Hughes, C. and Tight, M. (1998) *The Academic Career Handbook*. Buckingham: Open University Press.

Burgess, R.G. (1997) *Beyond the First Degree: Graduate Education, Lifelong Learning and Careers*. Buckingham: Open University Press.

Major, L.E. (1994) The doctors of debt, doubt and despondency. *The Times Higher Education Supplement*, 22 July, 6–7.

Neal, S. (1997) *The Making of Equal Opportunities Policies in Universities*. Buckingham: Open University Press.

Smith, A. and Webster, F. (eds) (1997) *The Postmodern University?* Buckingham: Open University Press.

References

Dane, F.C. (1990) *Research Methods*. Pacific Grove, CA: Brooks/Cole.

Parnes, S.J., Noller, R.B. and Biondi, A.M. (1977) *Guide to Creative Action: Revised Edition of Creative Behavior Guidebook*. New York: Scribner.

Sides, C.H. (1992) *How to Write and Present Technical Information*, 2nd edn. Cambridge: Cambridge University Press.

Index

Related books from Open University Press
Purchase from www.openup.co.uk or order through your local bookseller

THE RESEARCH STUDENT'S GUIDE TO SUCCESS
THIRD EDITION

Pat Cryer

A must read for all research students!

> The core material in Professor Cryer's previous editions is classic. I welcome this new edition setting it into current contexts.
>
> PhD supervisor

> When I was doing my own PhD, Pat Cryer's book was my constant reference companion. Now I am recommending her latest edition to my own students.
>
> PhD supervisor

Insightful, wide-ranging and accessible, this is an invaluable tool for postgraduate research students and for students at all levels working on research projects, irrespective of their field of study.

This edition has been thoroughly revised to accommodate the changes in postgraduate education over recent years. Additional material and new emphases take into account:

- the QAA Code of Practice for Postgraduate Research Programmes
- recommendations of the Roberts Review
- the needs of the growing number of 'overseas' research students
- employment issues (including undergraduate teaching)
- the Internet as a resource for research.

There are new chapters on:

- developing the research proposal
- succeeding as an 'overseas' research student
- ethics in research
- personal development planning (PDP)

Contents
List of figures – Preface to the third edition – Why and how to use this book – Exploring routes, opportunities and funding – Making an application – Producing the research proposal – Settling in and taking stock – Interacting with supervisors – Reading round the subject: working procedures – Reading round the subject: evaluating quality – Handling ethical issues – Managing influences of personal circumstances – Succeeding as an 'overseas' research student – Managing your skills development – Planning out the work – Getting into a productive routine – Co-operating with others for mutual support – Producing progress reports – Giving presentations on your work – Transferring registration from MPhil to PhD – Coming to terms with originality in research – Developing ideas through creative thinking – Keeping going when you feel like giving up – Job seeking – Producing the thesis – Handling the oral/viva/thesis defence – Afterwards! – Appendix: Skills training requirements for research students: Joint Statement by the UK Research Councils – Index.

2006   288pp
978–0–335–22117–2 (Paperback)   978–0–335–22118–9 (Hardback)

DOING YOUR RESEARCH PROJECT
FOURTH EDITION

Judith Bell

Worldwide bestseller - over 200,000 sold

An invaluable tool for anyone carrying out a research project.

We all learn to do research by actually doing it, but a great deal of time and effort can be wasted and goodwill lost by inadequate preparation. This book provides beginner researchers with the tools to do the job, to help them avoid some of the pitfalls and time-wasting false trails, and to establish good research habits. It takes researchers from the stage of choosing a topic through to the production of a well-planned, methodologically sound, and well-written final report or thesis on time. It is written in plain English and makes no assumptions about previous knowledge.

This new edition of *Doing Your Research Project* includes:

- New chapter on ethics
- Coverage of latest techniques such as grounded theory
- Completely updated coverage of documentary evidence
- Increased examples from health studies
- New referencing, library searching, and literature review chapters

This book is a guide to good practice for beginner researchers in any discipline embarking on undergraduate or postgraduate study, and for professionals in such fields as social science, education, and health.

Contents
*Preface to the fourth edition – Acknowledgements – Introduction – **PART I: Preparing the ground** – Approaches to research – Planning the project – Ethics and integrity in research – Reading, referencing and the management of information – Libraries and preparing for literature searches – The review of the literature – **PART II: Selecting methods of data collection** – The analysis of documentary evidence (written by Brendan Duffy) – Designing and administering questionnaires – Planning and conducting interviews – Diaries – Observation Studies – **PART III** – Interpreting the evidence and reporting the findings – Writing the report – Postscript – References – Index.*

2005   320pp
978–0–335–20660–5 (Paperback)   978–0–335–22418–0 (eBook)

HOW TO RESEARCH
THIRD EDITION

Loraine Blaxter, Christina Hughes and Malcolm Tight

Praise for the first edition:

> . . . an excellent choice for any student about to start a research project for the first time.
>
> *British Journal of Educational Technology*

Praise for the second edition:

> *How to Research* is best used as a reference tool to dip in and out of when required. Not only is it an excellent starting point for new researchers and students, but undoubtedly the more experienced researcher will also find it valuable. Furthermore, those involved in teaching research methods or supervising research students would find this a useful source of information, exercises and ideas.
>
> *SRA News*

How to Research is a practical handbook for those carrying out small scale research projects and discusses the practice and experience of doing research in the social sciences.

The new edition has been updated throughout and includes extensively revised chapters on introductory thinking about research and data analysis. Building on the strengths of the previous edition, Blaxter, Hughes and Tight include new material on:

- Writing research proposals
- Making presentations
- Researching in your own workplace
- Data collection software and time management
- Case studies of small scale research projects

It is written in an original, accessible and jargon free style using a variety of different forms of presentation to support the researcher. It is written for all those who are required to complete a research project as part of their studies and is invaluable for those conducting research in the workplace.

Contents

List of boxes – All at sea but learning to swim – Getting started – Thinking about methods – Reading for research – Managing your project – Collecting data – Analysing data – Writing up – Finishing off – References – Index.

2006   304pp
978–0–335–21746–5 (Paperback)   978–0–335–21747–2 (Hardback)